OLD QUILTS MADE NEW

OLD QUILTS MADE NEW

Finishing Antique Designs with Free Motion

TERESA DURYEA WONG

SCHIFFER CRAFT

4880 Lower Valley Road • Atglen, PA 19310

Other Schiffer Books by the Author:

Japanese Contemporary Quilts and Quilters: The Story of an American Import, ISBN 978-0-7643-4874-7

Magic & Memories: 45 Years of International Quilt Festival, ISBN 978-0-7643-5741-1

With Naomi Ichikawa: *Kawaii Appliqué Quilts from Japan: How One Country's Love of All Things Tiny Powers Today's Most Intricate Quilts*, ISBN 978-0-7643-6925-4

Other Schiffer Books on Related Subjects:

The Quilting Experience: A Celebration of Community and Patchwork Patterns, Victoria Findlay Wolfe, Foreword by Meg Cox, ISBN 978-0-7643-6807-3

Portable Patchwork: The Women Pioneers of the Original Quick & Easy Quilting Method, with Projects for Today, Pamela Weeks, ISBN 978-0-7643-6202-6

Commemorative American Quilts: Stitching Our Heritage from 1876 to Today, Sandra Sider, foreword by Pamela Weeks, ISBN 978-0-7643-7131-8

Library of Congress Control Number:2026932979

Designed by Lori Malkin Ehrlich
Cover design by Lindsay Hess
Front cover image: Detail, *Marie's World*. See page 47. Quilted by Teresa Duryea Wong.
Back cover images: Details from: (top) *Joe Wah's Feed Sacks*. See page 133. (right center) *Mrs. Wilson's First Grade Class*. See page 143. (bottom) *Mom's Folk Art Appliqué*. See page 137. All quilted by Teresa Duryea Wong.

Type set in Rig Sans / Circe / Laski Slab

ISBN: 978-0-7643-7245-2
ePub: 978-1-5073-0763-2
Printed in China

10 9 8 7 6 5 4 3 2 1

MIX
Paper | Supporting responsible forestry
FSC® C104723

Published by Schiffer Craft
An imprint of Schiffer Publishing, Ltd.
4880 Lower Valley Road
Atglen, PA 19310
Phone: (610) 593-1777; Fax: (610) 593-2002
Email: Info@schifferbooks.com
Web: www.schifferbooks.com

Dedicated to my best friend, the woman who taught me how to quilt, Amy Gurghigian.

Amy Gurghigian (*left*) and Teresa Duryea Wong with two hand-appliqué quilt tops we made together from a pattern by Kim McLean. Photographed in Jersey Village, Texas, 2010, by Christopher Wong.

CONTENTS

INTRODUCTION

Surfing the web one night from my pandemic couch, an antique quilt top caught my eye. I decided to buy it and finish it on my longarm sewing machine with free motion. I figured it would give me something to do in between making and finishing my own patchwork quilts.

When I create my own quilt tops, the process can take months, maybe even a year. With this old top that was already assembled and ready for finishing, there was something very satisfying about loading it on the machine right away and being able to start stitching the same day. After all, I have this machine. I love operating it. I thought, why not keep it busy?

This simple red, white, and blue patchwork is timeless. Photographed at Houston's Memorial Park Eastern Glades.

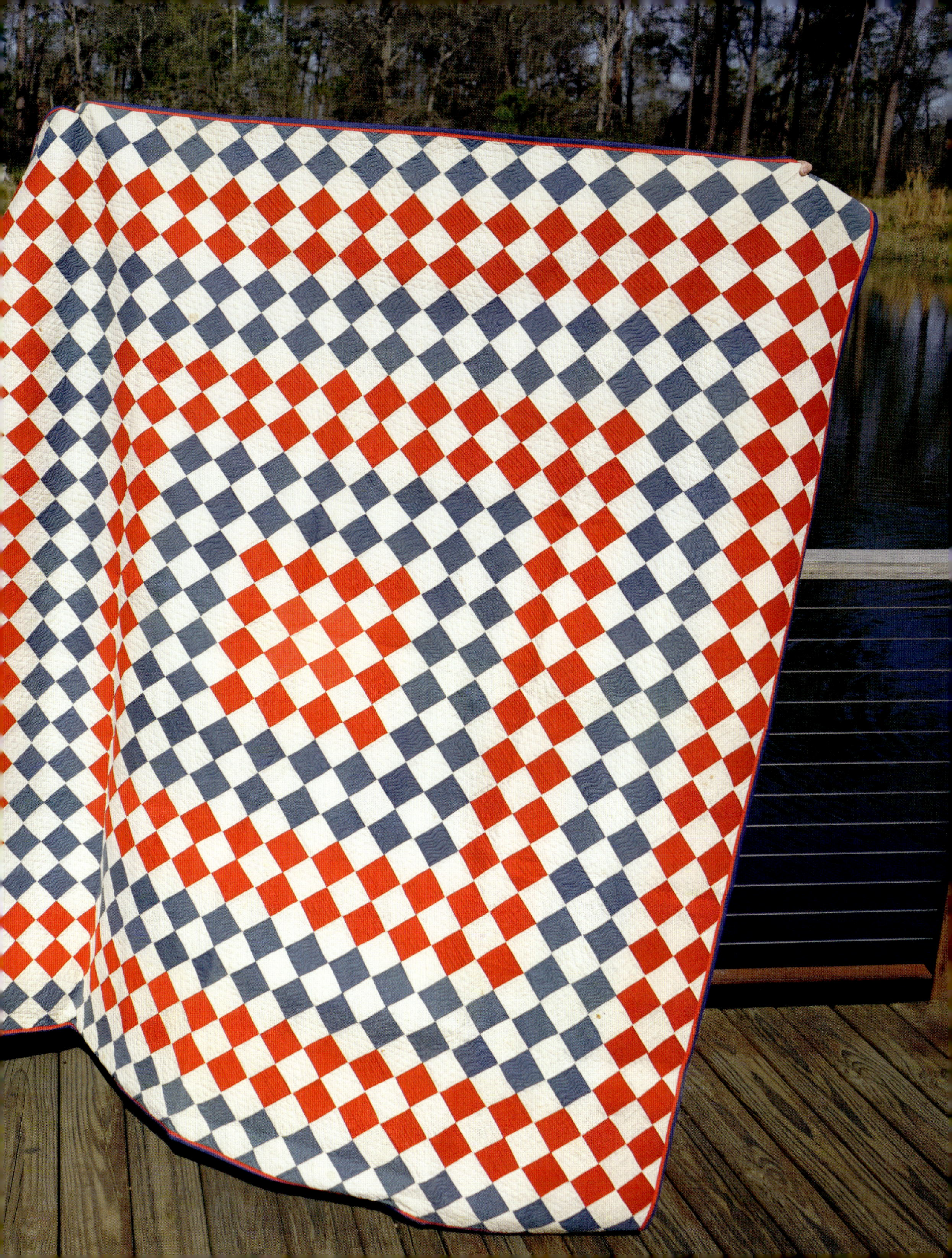

Sewing machines have been popular household appliances since the 1850s, but because most antique quilt tops were stitched by hand, quilters today feel an obligation to quilt them by hand as well. But modern sewing machines can actually bring beauty and life to these often-overlooked tops. Sewing machine photo by Azuree Holloway for *Quiltfolk* magazine.

Dozens of finished antique quilt tops later, I've certainly been keeping my machine and my hands busy. Each one is lovingly finished on modern equipment, and while I'm finishing these bits of sewn fabric, I think about the person who could have made this. Where did he or she live? What year was this made? Why didn't they finish it?

It is important to state up front that I do not use computerized quilting. Everything I quilt is executed with a machine that I am guiding with my own hands and sometimes with the help of acrylic rulers. In quilt world lingo, this technique is known as free motion.

I've shared my progress on Instagram, and I've exhibited eleven of these quilts at the International Quilt Festival in Houston in 2024 and again at the International Quilt Museum in Lincoln, Nebraska, in 2025. The vast majority of comments and feedback I have received applaud my effort to rescue these quilt tops. I'm proud that they are finally finished. But to be honest, the act of rescuing was not my goal. Rather, my goal was to create opportunities to apply my free-motion quilting skills. That may not be the answer you would expect. But, in reality, I began this project in order to enjoy the process of machine quilting, and as a result, I have indeed saved quite a few quilt tops.

Adding creative free-motion quilting to old tops brings new life to these antique treasures that might otherwise never see the light of day.

OPPOSITE, TOP: A close-up of this Ocean Waves pattern shows how a modern ¼-inch grid can create an updated look for this classic design.

OPPOSITE, BOTTOM: An unusual six-pointed star with a pieced hexagon center is named after my paternal grandfather.

IF QUILTS COULD TALK

As a quilt researcher, I've found that there is nothing more satisfying than exploring a quilt's history and the role it played in the lives of humans. There are countless incredible stories about quilts and their makers. A case in point—the nonprofit Quilt Alliance has collected some 1,200 recorded oral histories of American quilters and their stories. These priceless documentations are preserved and stored at the Library of Congress and the University of Kentucky, and they are searchable and open to everyone on the Quilt Alliance Quilters Save Our Stories (QSOS) website.

A special exhibition of eleven quilts at the International Quilt Festival quilts titled *Finally Finished*. Houston, 2024. Photo by Jimmy Wong.

The twenty-one quilt tops featured on these pages that I have finished have no oral history and no story whatsoever. We do not know who made them or why they made them. We don't know when they were made exactly; we can only guess by studying the fabrics. We don't know if the maker was happy to make it, or if it was drudgery. We don't know if the maker was a pioneer woman sitting in a rocking chair or possibly a wealthy woman in Baltimore. And there are so many other possibilities that are often overlooked in quilt history narratives, and not all stories are romantic. For example, an antique quilt top from the 1800s could have been made by an enslaved person who labored without enjoyment. Or, it could have been made by a young Indigenous girl who was forced to attend a boarding school, far away from her family, and forced by

missionaries to spend her days sewing and making quilts. It could have been made during the Depression era, during a family's most difficult moments. There is no way to know.

So, in the absence of information, I opted to create my own narratives, because in my world, every quilt deserves a story. I named this set of quilts after my relatives and family who have passed away, and for individuals (and even a horse) who played memorable roles in my life. In some of these stories, I matched the quilt's attributes to the person it is named after.

For example, my brother's childhood bedroom was decorated in red, white, and blue, so the plain red-and-blue one-patch is named after him. A Barn Raising quilt made me think of hell-raising, which made me think of my dad. So, he gets the Hell Raising Barn Raising title. And the antique quilt blocks I finished with machine embroidery are named after Mrs. Holly, who lived next door to us when I was in second grade and taught me how to embroider.

Creating these narratives added a new twist to the process of finishing these quilts, and it was rewarding to think about the important people in my life while I was quilting. I consider this idea as an extension of the creative process. Whether real or imagined, I love that these finished quilts now have a story. I hope you enjoy reading about how I finished these quilts, as well as the stories of people in my life whom I am honoring by naming one of these quilts after them.

ANTIQUE QUILT TOPS FINISHED WITH FREE MOTION

In my world, every quilt deserves a story.

Vintage top created with feed sacks. Photographed in Brenham, Texas.

JOOST & THE CHIMNEY SWEEP

BLOCK PATTERN: Chimney Sweep. Brackman #3266.

QUILT TOP: Circa 1870–1890. Hand-pieced.

PURCHASED: eBay, January 2022. $285.00.

FABRIC: Cotton & muslin

BATTING: Warm & Natural 100% cotton

QUILTING THREAD: Superior Kimono Silk 100 wt.

BACKING: Wide backing. Judie Rothermel reproduction cotton paisley print. Purchased circa 2000, then sat for twenty-five years waiting for the perfect top.

DIMENSIONS: 86 × 74 in. (221 × 188 cm)

How'd You Quilt That?

Silk Thread

Silk is a perfect choice because it glides gently and it's a natural fiber. Be sure to use a needle appropriate for finer thread. I use a 70/10 or 60/8 needle because a smaller eye is needed with such a thin thread. When threading the needle, I run the thread over a tiny felt pad that is installed on my machine, near where the thread is inserted, to help support this thin thread. Most modern machines include this extra tool.

A Note About Natural Fibers

You will notice that my choices for batting, thread, and fabric are only natural fibers. Many people use synthetic threads or batting, and that is a personal choice. Synthetic threads come in beautiful colors and specialties. However, I never use synthetic threads or batting. I believe that natural fibers are the best way to honor the quilts and create them with sustainable materials.

Subtle Design

If you want a subtle quilting design, silk thread is an excellent choice because from afar, you will see texture, but the quilting motif is not immediately obvious. This beautiful, thin thread is so elegant. You can see the texture it adds, but the stitching does not overpower the patchwork.

Motif

The quilting design used here is not dense but adds circular movement to these angular blocks. I used acrylic longarm rulers to create precise circles and curves. The swirl in the red corners is free motion.

TIP: Study the patchwork and choose a quilting design that enhances the original patchwork rather than one that covers it up. This is the best way to honor the maker and create harmony with the old top and new stitching.

MY PROJECT to finish antique quilt tops all started with Joost, in the same way that part of the Duryea lineage in America included Joost Duryea (sometimes spelled Durie or Duryee). He was a French Huguenot who born in France in 1635 and later moved to Mannheim, Germany.

At the age of forty, Joost brought his wife, Magdalena; his mother; and four sons from his first marriage to America and settled in New Utrecht, Long Island (in an area that is now Brooklyn). He established a farm there and is considered one of the original settlers of Long Island.

He sold his farm in 1681 and moved to a "disputed" territory between Bushwick and Newton, and this is where he built the family homestead and lived the remainder of his life. The home he built on this property was torn down in 1903 to make room for the railroad, and the destruction was reported in the *New York Sun* newspaper. Joost and Magdalena had seven children in this house. After Magdalena died, Joost married again, and his third wife was named Cornelia. He died in 1727 at the age of eighty-eight.

Joost's story is especially fascinating to me because my daughter moved to New York City in 2011, and for a while she lived in Brooklyn. We visit Manhattan and Brooklyn often, so I'm certain that at some point we've walked along the same ground that Joost once farmed.

City. It is the original homestead of the Duryea family whose progenitor was Joost Durié.

on the ship Otter on Feb. 17, 1659, he probably never thought that his descendants would prosper here under the name of De

ORIGINAL HOME OF THE DURYEAS AND DURYEES.

He was a French Huguenot and came from Mannheim in the Palatinate. After coming here the family became connected

Bevoise. He was a well-educated French Protestant, and previous to coming to this country lived at Leyden in Holland.

TOP: Late-nineteenth-century quilt photographed in Chappell Hill, Texas.
ABOVE: In 1903, the *New York Sun* reported the destruction of Joost Duryea's home, which had stood for two hundred years.

GRANDMOTHER PEARL'S FLOWER GARDEN

BLOCK PATTERN: Grandmother's Flower Garden. Brackman #160L.

QUILT TOP: Circa 1930s. Hand-pieced.

PURCHASED: eBay, April 2023. $160.00.

FABRIC: Cotton, shirting scraps, some feed sacks

BATTING: Warm & Natural 100% cotton

QUILTING THREAD: Aurifil cotton 50 wt.

BACKING: Wide backing. Colorful fireworks design set on black.

DIMENSIONS: 75 × 96 in. (191 × 244 cm)

The classic design is always delightful, and it looks even better when it's hung outside on a picket fence, on a sunny day, with flowers. Photographed at Havenly Farm, Fulshear, Texas.

How'd You Quilt That?

Multiple Thread Colors to Match the Patchwork

I used multiple colors of cotton thread to complement each hexagon. I chose yellow cotton thread in the bobbin. Sometimes I prefer to change the bobbin thread to match the top thread color, but for this one I opted to use just one bobbin color. There is no right or wrong choice for the bobbin thread color.

A Design for Each Patch

This top was in excellent condition, and it was fun to quilt. All the stitching in this quilt is free motion except the centers of each flower garden. These are matchstick quilted in straight lines, using a ruler and white thread.

I quilted a swirl in each of the yellow border hexies in matching yellow thread. Because I work on a longarm machine, I was able to start on one side of the quilt and go all the way across the quilt and stitch most of the yellow hexies without starting and stopping in each patch. The hexies surrounding the center are quilted in various ribbon motif designs. I was able to stitch the ring of hexies in each block without starting and stopping in each small hexie patch.

Matching the thread color to the fabric brings texture to the quilt without distracting from the original patchwork.

TIP: Starting and stopping on each patch can be tedious. I look for motifs that allow me to stitch longer sections in one continuous motion. If you need to backtrack or jump over one patch to keep the motion going, you can always "stitch in the ditch" of a neighboring patch in order to reposition the machine for the next stretch.

PEARL RILEY BACON was my paternal great-grandmother. She lived in Dawson, Nebraska. Later in life, possibly while living at the nursing home, she made several quilts that are part of my collection. Pearl died while I was still young, so I do not remember much about her. I think she would have liked this quilt, with its strong colors and precise piecing.

This Grandmother's Flower Garden quilt top caught my attention because of the bold yellow hexies bordering each of the flower garden blocks. I love the fabrics that were chosen for this top; they are a mix of cotton prints, plus shirting fabric that was most certainly left over from garment sewing, as well as feed sacks.

My paternal great-grandmother Pearl Riley Bacon.

SHIRT SCRAPS JK WONG WOULD LOVE

BLOCK PATTERN: The Dewey. Brackman #2473.

QUILT TOP: Date unknown. Hand-pieced.

PURCHASED: Round Top, Texas, antique fair. 2024. $18.00.

FABRIC: Cotton, shirting scraps

BATTING: Warm & Natural 100% cotton

QUILTING THREAD: Aurifil cotton 50 wt.

BACKING: Pieced. Japanese woven fabric scraps in taupe palette.

DIMENSIONS: 41 × 41 in. (104 × 104 cm)

How'd You Quilt That?

Creating Pattern for Interest

This is a small quilt, and, studying the textiles, it appears to be quite old. Some of these fabrics appear to be scraps from men's shirts, which I think gives this quilt a wonderful masculine vibe.

Since these blocks are created improvisationally, the quilt top is imperfect. The large border fabric just seemed to need something extra, so I created a stitched pattern on each side. I created a row, almost like a flowing ribbon, across each side by stitching two sets of close wavy lines. These were done free motion, so they are imperfect too. Then I stitched the bubble motif outside these wavy lines.

TIP: These borders are a great example of how you can create your own graphic patterns inside a large space like this. When I choose a top to finish, I look for wide-open spaces like these where I can add something to the design. These borders were the perfect opportunity to do just that. Instead of stitching one motif across the whole border, you can break up the sections by adding your graphic design like this example, then stitch in and around those designs to create something interesting.

The Dewey Block

This was not a block name I was familiar with. According to the *Brackman Encyclopedia of Pieced Quilt Patterns*, this block is named The Dewey. These blocks have interesting lines because of the imperfect piecing. I stitched simple straight lines in the long rectangles and triangles, matchstick lines in the center squares, and stippling with small loops on the negative-space patches.

AFTER HIS FOURTH CHILD was born, JK Wong, my father-in-law, left his small village in South China and found work as a merchant marine. He traveled the world, working on ships while saving every cent he could for his dream—moving to America and bringing over his entire family.

In the late 1940s, he did in fact immigrate to America. He moved to Mississippi to be close to where his sister lived. A decade later, he began bringing his family over and eventually his four children and their spouses and children; many other distant relatives and friends were also brought here under his sponsorship and support. Even to this day, my husband and I meet people who tell us stories about how JK helped them leave China and move to Houston.

JK was very social and always a snappy dresser. This small quilt, with all these leftover shirting fabrics, could have easily come from his own wardrobe of button-down shirts.

RIGHT: My father-in-law, JK Wong, circa 1950s.

OPPOSITE: Photographed in the historic downtown Brenham, Texas.

131
133
135
137

EUGENE: BARN RAISING & HELL RAISING

BLOCK PATTERN: Log Cabin. Brackman #2574.

QUILT PATTERN: Barn Raising

QUILT TOP: Circa 1900. Hand-pieced.

PURCHASED: eBay, March 2023. $499.00.

FABRIC: Cotton

BATTING: Warm & Natural 100% cotton

QUILTING THREAD: Aurifil cotton 50 wt.

BACKING: Pieced. Reproduction print of old New York signage (*center*) and woven border fabric, both made in Japan.

DIMENSIONS: 85 × 86 in. (216 × 218 cm)

How'd You Quilt That?

Embrace the Simple

These blocks are improv pieced—each block is a different size. There was no attempt for precision when this quilt was assembled, and that makes this quilt atypical, because Barn Raising patterns are usually precise.

This quilting motif is very simple, just two straight lines inside each patch. In this case, simple was the best way to finish a quilt without detracting from the dark and light overall pattern.

I used dark-blue thread in the dark areas, and cream thread in the light areas. The stitching is all free hand, no rulers. I did not want straight lines, since this quilt is somewhat improvisational and there are no perfectly straight lines in the patchwork.

Each block has a red center, and these are quilted in red thread, with a swirl design.

The binding is a red/tan Kaffe Fassett woven stripe, which has the look of an old fabric.

Fabric Dating via Instagram

When the quilt top arrived, I noticed it had quite a few ripples and waves. I had to fix two blocks that had big wavy problems; the rest I quilted as is. There are prints in this quilt that I have never seen, and originally I thought this quilt was possibly made in the mid-1800s. But when I posted it on Instagram, noted antique quilt expert Julie Silber commented that the fabric dates this quilt to the end of the nineteenth century, most likely between 1880 and the early 1900s. I love learning with the help of social media! The information comes in immediately, and you can reach out to so many knowledgeable people.

A LOG CABIN pattern organized like this quilt (with dark and light sections forming diamond-shaped designs) is called a Barn Raising quilt. When I purchased it, I got to thinking about barn raising, which led me to think about my dad, who certainly excelled at hell-raising. So, I named this one for him.

Eugene Jay Duryea was born on March 17, 1934, and died on June 29, 2005. He was a true character, an original in every sense of the word. Eugene Jay, or Jay as he was known, always followed his passion. He raced sailboats, flew airplanes, golfed, and loved a great party.

He served in the Air Force during the Korean War, but not as a professional pilot. Rather, he was sent to language school in California and then later to Europe, where his job was to translate military messages from German to English. In a fascinating sidenote, my brother-in-law Arnold Fong, who grew up in China and moved to America as a child, also served during the Korean War and was sent to the same military language school as my dad, possibly around the same time. Arnold was eventually sent to the DMZ (demilitarized zone between North and South Korea), where he translated Chinese (probably both Mandarin and Cantonese) to English. Family histories are fascinating!

Back to my dad, flying was always something he wanted to do, especially since both his brothers were pilots. After his military service, he earned a private pilot's license, and for many years he owned a small, single-engine plane. He cherished the time he spent flying that plane.

My favorite thing to do during most of my dad's plane rides was to fall fast asleep as soon as possible. These days, I'm especially grateful that at least on one of our flights back in 1987, I had the smarts to bring along my camera and capture this photo of him in flight while the sun is setting on the horizon.

ABOVE: My father, Eugene Jay Duryea, flying his plane, 1987.
RIGHT: Photographed at Havenly Farm, Fulshear, Texas.

MARIE'S WORLD

BLOCK PATTERN: Mountain Mist #30 Cross Purposes pattern (with some variation).

QUILT TOP: Circa 1920s–30s (possibly). Hand-pieced.

PURCHASED: Xenia Cord's Legacy Quilts. International Quilt Festival, Houston, 2022. $125.00.

FABRIC: Cotton & muslin

BATTING: Warm & Plush 100% cotton

QUILTING THREAD: Aurifil cotton 50 wt.

BACKING: Wide backing. Pink Kona cotton.

DIMENSIONS: 89 × 89 in. (226 × 226 cm)

How'd You Quilt That?

Make Boring Beautiful

The large muslin inner borders seemed extremely boring, but I saw them as the perfect opportunity to create my own pattern and texture. I used rulers, free motion, and several different thread colors to stitch an intricate graphic pattern. The mix of repetitive, precise shapes created by the rulers, combined with the imprecise free motion, makes this a compelling motif. The quilting is very dense. From afar, these borders almost look like a printed fabric rather than stitching.

Honor the Patchwork

Again, as you will see in many of these quilts, I have chosen to quilt one individual motif that is contained within each patch. This technique enhances the design without distracting from the color and pattern of the print. It also stays true to the original pattern of the blocks and overall design.

Never Give Up! A Tuck Here, a Tuck There.

This quilt is a lesson on how to never give up. The piecing in the patchwork was not that accurate, and the quilt did not lie flat. I tried flattening it with the iron and steam before loading it on the longarm frame. My plan was to flatten the wavy areas as I quilted it. As you might guess, this rarely works, and I do not recommend this approach. I got so frustrated with this quilt that I took it off the frame and set it aside. When I finally came back to it several weeks later, I was determined to make it work.

My solution was unconventional, and many would say unprofessional. At two different points on this quilt top, I pinched the excess wavy fabric and made a tuck that enabled the wavy areas to lie flat. Then I ironed the tucked areas and stitched right over them as if they did not exist. To be honest, there was a lot of angst during this process, and even some cussing along the way. Of course, even though the tucks were small, the pattern did not line up after I did this. I worried that it would look awful, but I was determined to finish this quilt. I figured that finished was better than perfect. I also learned a valuable lesson! For the next old quilt top, I made sure it was flat, or repaired to be flat, before quilting it.

Now that the quilt is complete, and because of the dense quilting over the whole thing, the tucks are barely noticeable. I am extremely proud of the finished quilt, and I hope that by sharing my unconventional solution, it will encourage other makers to never give up!

An unorthodox solution for a quilt that refused to lie flat.

THIS QUILT IS NAMED after my maternal grandmother, Marie Freiburg Lennemann. She was a nurse and married a doctor, Ernest "Doc" Lennemann. Doc was a country doctor who routinely made house calls. He delivered almost every baby in Richardson County, Nebraska, including my father!

After retirement, my grandparents traveled all over the world, and Marie always sent me postcards from their trips. My family never traveled, unless you call driving thirteen hours from Texas to Nebraska to visit relatives traveling. So, Marie's world seemed so exotic to me. I was fascinated by those postcards and the glimpses of the faraway places and the messages she sent just to me.

Marie was known to be an excellent seamstress. Her cabinet Singer sewing machine was set up in the living room. My mom watched her sew on that machine nearly every day, and now I have that machine in my own home. This photo was taken at Christmas in 1968 at the home where they retired to in Medicine Lake, Idaho.

This quilt has ideas similar to the Trip Around the World pattern, which made me think of Marie and her travels. However, this design is a slight variation of a Mountain Mist pattern #30 titled Cross Purposes.

TOP: My maternal grandmother, Marie Freiburg Lennemann.

MIDDLE: Marie's Singer sewing machine sits in my home today.

LEFT: Doc and Marie Lennemann at their retirement cabin in Medicine Lake, Idaho, in 1968.

OPPOSITE: A historic building in the Houston Heights neighborhood is the perfect temporary backdrop.

NEOLA & NO SPIDER WEBS

BLOCK PATTERN: Spider Web. Brackman #1306.

QUILT TOP: Circa 1910 (according to dealer). Hand-pieced.

PURCHASED: eBay, March 2023. $135.00.

FABRIC: Cotton, linen, woven ticking fabric, cotton prints

BATTING: Warm & Natural 100% cotton

QUILTING THREAD: Aurifil cotton 50 wt.

BACKING: Pieced. American Made Brand solid burgundy cotton.

DIMENSIONS: 72 × 80 in. (183 × 203 cm)

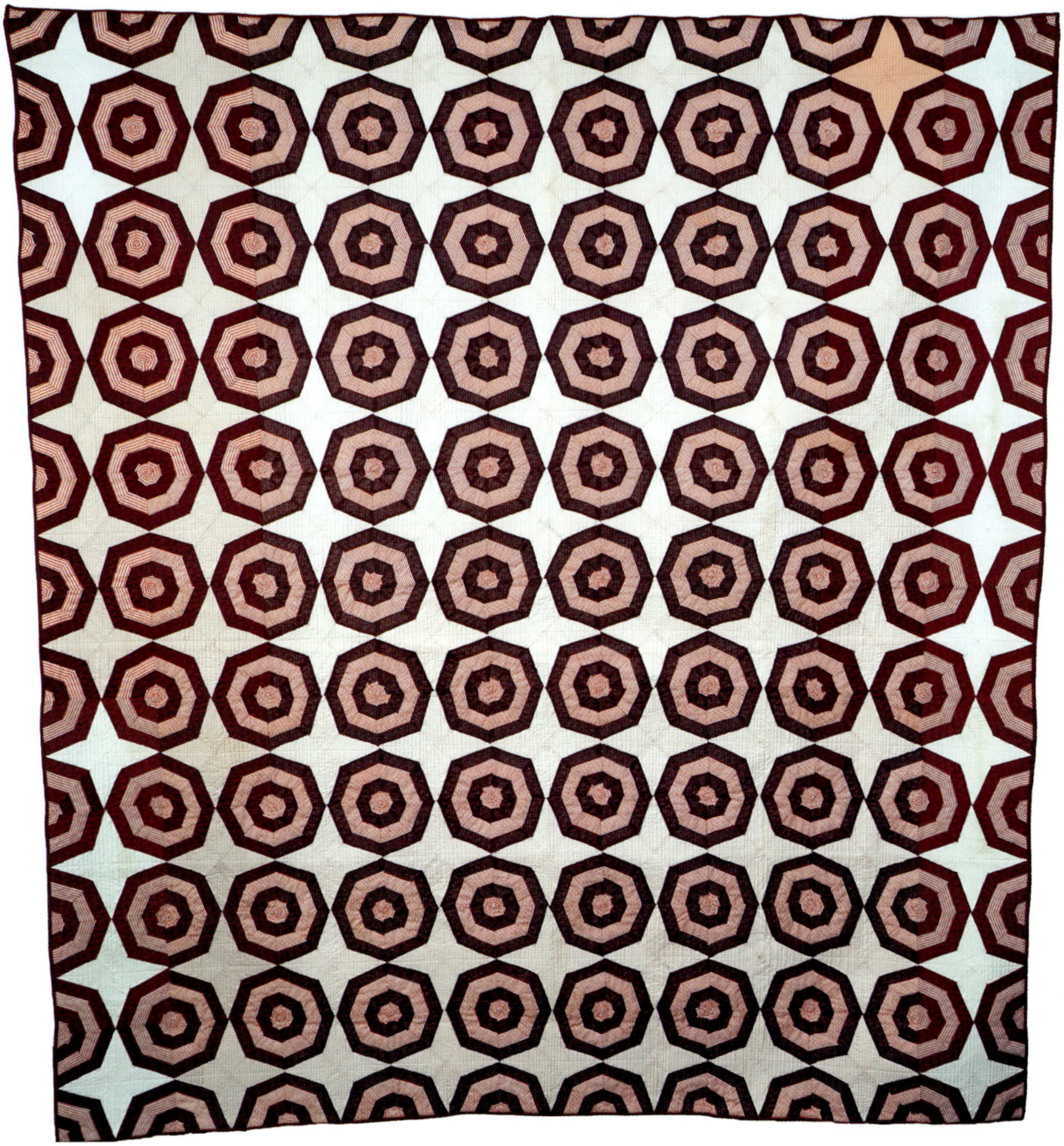

How'd You Quilt That?

When I saw this quilt for sale online, I was immediately drawn to the wonkiness of these octagon blocks. They are burgundy solid, with a row of red/white ticking, then another round of burgundy, and ticking in the centers. The outer two rows appear to be added on later because they are made from a deeper burgundy solid cotton. The maker of this quilt is my kind of woman (possibly a man), because she just had fun making this top and didn't worry about the rules of matching points and lines.

This top is an excellent example of thinking about what to quilt and what not to quilt. Sometimes, leaving a certain section unquilted can make it stand out and create a more dynamic overall design.

For the outer row of ticking, I opted to leave these as is and did not quilt over them. I felt that the choice to use ticking fabric was unusual (even though some blocks are made with a commercial print that mimics ticking). Ticking harkens back to a time when this durable, woven fabric served very specific purposes, and I wanted it to stand out on the finished quilt.

Besides the wonky blocks, the other thing that appealed to me with this quilt was the off-white solid negative spaces, which look like four-pointed stars, between each block. I felt that these open spaces were a great opportunity to create matchstick lines that would add texture and not detract from the overall bold design of this quilt. There is just one star that is pieced with a soft, peach-colored fabric, and I just love that choice. We have to wonder: Did the maker run out of her off-white fabric? Or was this just a punch of creativity to keep us all guessing? In either case, that lovely negative space is matchstick quilted in a matching thread color.

NEOLA DURYEA PROUDFIT was my dad's cousin. Neola was the only child of Seth and Agnes Duryea and was born in Nims City (near Dawson) in 1917. The family later moved to Bern, Kansas. She and William "Bill" Morrow Proudfit were married in 1941. Neola attended Kansas State University and was a schoolteacher before she got married. Bill and Neola had been childhood friends, but Bill's parents moved away, and the two reconnected at college. Bill became an industrial engineer, and at some point they moved to Houston.

I have so many vivid memories of visiting with Neola and Bill at their home in Houston. The home was gorgeous and always immaculately clean. When I learned that this quilt block pattern's name is Spider Web, it seemed fitting to name this quilt *Neola & No Spider Webs.*

Neola was always beautifully dressed, her hair was always styled, and as I remember, she was always smiling. She was an easy person to be around, and I loved being the little kid in the background while she and my parents visited. They played bridge (a card game) together for many years, and there was always a lot of drinking, smoking, laughter, and talking. Neola passed away in 2013 at the age of ninety-seven.

I named this quilt for Neola so I could remember her fun personality and gracious smile. I doubt that Neola sewed, but maybe she did. I would guess that if she were to ever make a quilt, it would not be wonky like this one. But still, I think she would have appreciated having this unique, imperfect quilt with its artsy aesthetic named after her.

LEFT: This photo is from our wedding. Neola is on the right, with my grandmother Frances (*middle*), and Bill Proudfit (*left*).

RIGHT: Photographed outside Tea Time Quilting, a longtime staple in Houston's Heights neighborhood.

Tea Time
QUILTING
AROUND THE CORNER ON TULANE

RACE TO VERACRUZ

BLOCK PATTERN: Sailboats. Brackman #912.

QUILT TOP: Date unknown. Hand-pieced.

PURCHASED: Round Top, Texas antique fair, 2024. $45.00

FABRIC: Cotton

BATTING: Warm & Natural 100% cotton

QUILTING THREAD: Aurifil cotton 40 wt.

BACKING: Pieced. Vintage heavy cotton tablecloth with solid red borders.

DIMENSIONS: 75 × 85 in. (191 × 216 cm)

Photographed in Seabrook, Texas.

How'd You Quilt That?

Borrowing a Technique from Art Quilts

When I first unfolded this top at a booth at the Round Top, Texas, antique fair, I immediately saw potential to create a big design in the negative spaces around these sailboats. I loved the boats, but I thought there was room to add more interest.

So, I opted to borrow a technique from art quilts—thread painting. This technique allows you to create patterns, shapes, or objects like this sun and star entirely from thread. I started by marking the outline of the shape on the fabric. Then I stitched within that shape over and over until the space was covered in several layers of thread. This requires a lot of patience because it takes time to fill an empty space completely with a single line of thread.

Thread painting will definitely change the hand of the fabric. The area that is so heavily stitched will become stiff and might even bow in or out. Those issues did not bother me, since this is not a quilt that will be utilitarian.

Create Your Own Unique Borders

The maker kept this quilt simple, with white sashing and white in all the negative spaces. I wanted to see more pattern in the plain sashing, so I created an original design by stitching half circles on the top and bottom of the sashing. The top and bottom half circles were carefully lined up so they would intersect. Then I filled those half circles with a ribbon motif.

Fun with Boats

Using free motion, I stitched a clamshell pattern along the bottom of each boat, in an attempt to reference waves. Then I stitched long, wavy lines across the hull, and stippling with small loops over the sails. The white negative-space patches around the sails are stitched with simple straight lines.

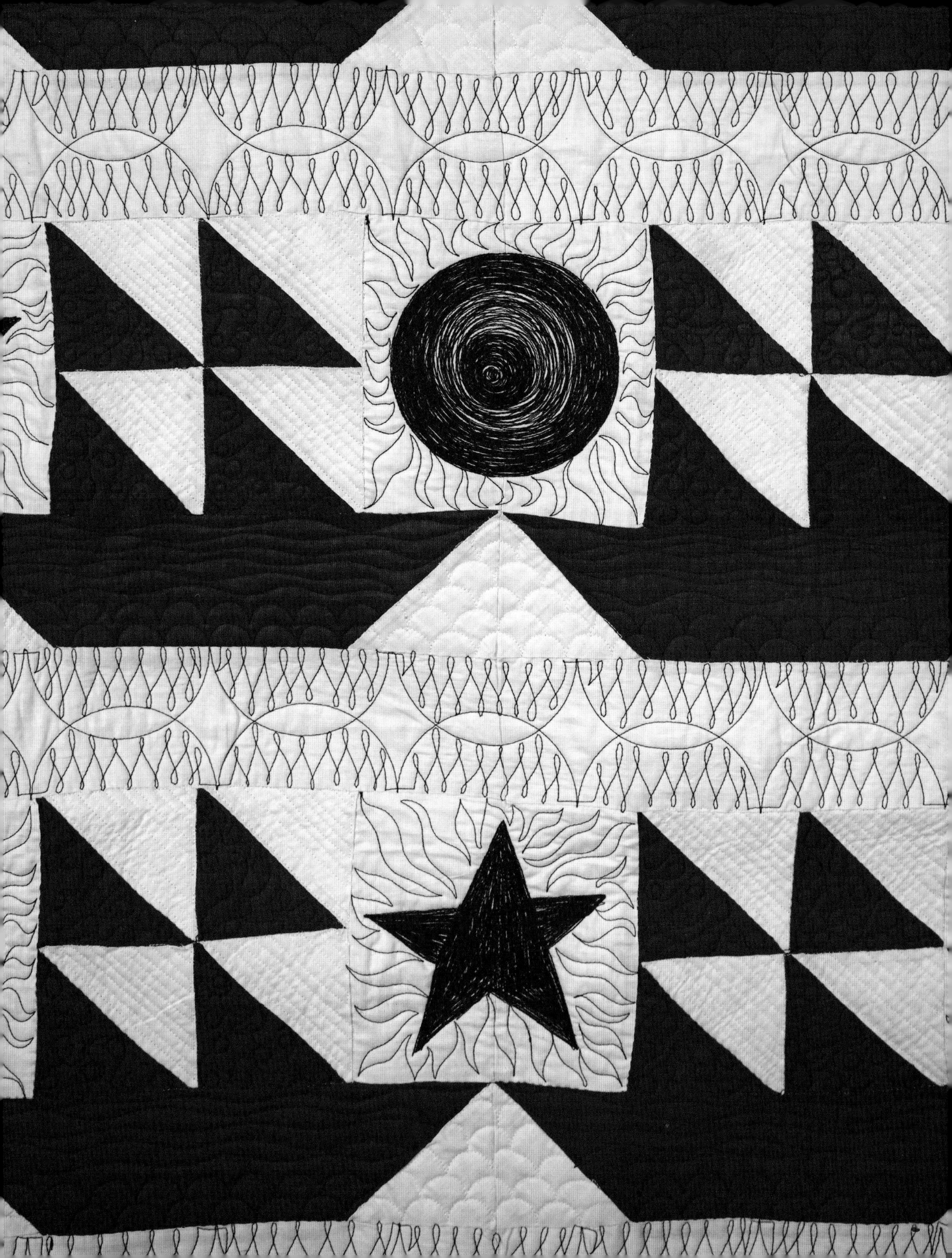

MY FATHER loved racing sailboats, and for many years in the late 1960s he participated in Regata de Amigos, an offshore race from Galveston, Texas to Veracruz, Mexico.

Tourism agencies in both countries, along with the US and Mexican governments, partnered to organize this sailboat race, which began in 1961. One summer in the late 1960s, my mom and a family friend drove me and my brother and sister to South Padre Island, at the border with Mexico, to meet my dad after the race ended. We all boarded my dad's sailboat for a leisurely trip back to Galveston Bay, and the family friend drove the car back to Houston.

This trip was the only childhood trip we ever had that resembled a vacation. Every other trip was to visit relatives. Even though we often sailed together as a family, we usually stayed close to home in Galveston Bay. So, this trip was exciting. I remember almost everything. The first leg of the trip was in rough water, and it was scary, plus I got seasick. After that, we sailed along the intercoastal waterway, which was as smooth as glass.

This photo was taken on my dad's sailboat when I was just a toddler, while sailing in Galveston Bay in the Gulf of Mexico.

CECIL'S SIX-POINTED STAR

BLOCK PATTERN: Six-pointed star. Brackman #3718 with a pieced hexagon center.

QUILT TOP: Circa 1870s. Hand-pieced.

PURCHASED: eBay, March 16, 2023. $87.94.

FABRIC: Cotton prints, silk, cotton solids

BATTING: Warm & Natural 100% cotton

QUILTING THREAD: Superior Kimono Silk 100 wt.

BACKING: Pieced. Commercial cotton print, reproduction leafy vine design.

DIMENSIONS: 73 × 86 in. (185 × 218 cm)

These six-pointed stars shine in Wimberley, Texas.

How'd You Quilt That?

Silk Thread, Simple Motif

Silk thread is gentle and beautiful. Each point of this unusual six-point star is stitched with a simple line about a ¼ inch from the edge. The motif on this quilt is deliberately simple, in order to allow this very old patchwork to shine.

Negative Space Opens Opportunity

The deep-red/maroon hexies in the negative space really make this top extraordinary. The red color does not seem to have faded over time.

Each hexie is stitched with a simple design that references a rose. To create this pattern, begin with a single line connecting the middle of one edge of the hexie to the middle of the edge next to it. Continue creating straight lines from the middle of each new line to the one next to it. The straight lines will get progressively shorter until you reach the center.

Silk Centers Left Untouched

The choice of these red silk centers in each block is surprising. They actually resemble a Japanese silk kimono print and could have been imported. Another theory is they could be an American-made silk designed in an Asian style, which would have been a popular fashion choice at the time. I chose not to add stitching in these centers because I wanted to honor this original, unexpected fabric choice and not distract from it.

I was attracted to this quilt top because of the incredibly vivid deep, reddish blocks in between the four-pointed stars. The muted color palette of the prints, and limited number of colors in each print, seems to suggest fabrics that were produced during and after the Civil War, and even into the early 1900s. The majority of prints are two colors only; a few prints are three colors.

CECIL PAUL DURYEA, who was always known by his nickname, "Crip," was my paternal grandfather. He was born on July 16, 1899, on a homestead in Richardson County, Nebraska, and died in 1986. He married my grandmother, Frances Irene Riley, on June 23, 1923, in Council Bluffs, Iowa.

ABOVE: Both of my paternal grandparents worked for the Lincoln Telegraph and Telephone Company in Nebraska. This photo was most likely taken by the company, or a newspaper photographer, when a home operator unit was installed in their home in the small town of Dawson, Nebraska. My grandmother was a professional telephone operator for many years, and I still remember her sitting there connecting one caller to another with a series of wires.

Throughout my life, both of my grandparents expected us to call them by their first names, so we never knew them as Grandma or Grandpa, but rather as Frances and Crip.

We spent a lot of time together, even though we lived in two different states. Frances and Crip came to visit us in Texas quite often, once or twice a year. And our family, along with my Uncle Don and my cousins, visited our grandparents in Nebraska every summer and Christmas. Fifteen people in a small house with one bathroom!

I always remember Crip sitting in his chair in front of the TV, smoking and reading the newspaper. His main job, as far back as I can remember, was to do the dishes after dinner. He and Frances fought like cats and dogs, always yelling at each other. When dinner was done, he'd put on an apron and go to work in the kitchen. When Frances would bark orders at him, he would salute her and say, "Yes, ma'am!"

As a young man, Crip worked in the family car repair business. He was also an excellent baseball player. He served in the Army Air Corp during WWI in Texas and was sent to England. During WWII, he worked for Martin Air Craft in Omaha as a line foreman, where he helped build B-26 and B-29 aircraft (the B-29 was the bomber that dropped the atomic bombs in Japan). After WWII ended, he returned to Dawson and Lincoln, where he worked for Lincoln Telegraph and Telephone Company until he retired in 1966.

I named this quilt for him because it definitely looks like something he would have had in his bedroom, and the era of this quilt is something that could have been made by his own mother, or even his grandmother.

My paternal grandfather, Cecil Paul Duryea, in a portrait most likely taken before his wedding in 1923.

UNCLE DON'S JAZZY JOSEPH COAT

BLOCK PATTERN: Joseph's Coat, a.k.a. Rainbow Bars, or Bars. Brackman #475.

QUILT TOP: Circa 1920s. Machine-pieced.

PURCHASED: eBay, July 2024. $245.00. Dealer purchased it from an auction house in Lancaster County, Pennsylvania. Believed to have been made in the Amish community.

FABRIC: Thin cotton, possibly batiste. Possibly hand-dyed.

BATTING: Warm & Natural 100% cotton

QUILTING THREAD: Superior Kimono Silk 100 wt. Matching colors.

BACKING: Wide backing. Yellow Kona cotton.

DIMENSIONS: 75 × 76 in. (191 × 193 cm)

How'd You Quilt That?

Simple, Simple, Simple

This quilt is all about the bold graphic pattern. Any attempt to add heavy pattern with fancy stitching would totally detract from the strong visuals. So, I simply quilted straight lines in matching silk threads.

The border is matchstick quilted. The bars are stitched across with single lines in a repeating pattern for each bar. For example, two sets of two lines for blue, five close lines for the yellow, and so on.

MY UNCLE Don Riley Duryea was the middle child of three boys born to Frances and Cecil Paul "Crip" Duryea. And as it often goes with the middle kid, he couldn't have been more different than his two brothers, my dad and my Uncle Paul. He was born in Dawson, Nebraska, in 1928 and died in 2004.

Don was both a gifted jazz musician and a painter. He served in the Army during WWII and was assigned to the US Army dance band and stationed in New Orleans.

When I was in elementary school, Don and his Market Square Jazz Band performed on Thursday nights at a nightclub called Hubers that was located in the Old Market Square in downtown Houston. My family was there nearly every week. I have such vivid memories of that wonderful music and all the adults talking and partying. Don played both clarinet and saxophone.

As a painter and professional graphic artist, he always had plenty of art supplies around his home. And each time we visited, I always went straight to his studio area and spent my time doodling. In fact, every time I quilt bubble stitches into my quilts, it reminds me of the endless hours I spent filling patterns with tiny circles at my Uncle Don's house.

I think he would have loved the bold graphics of this quilt known as a Joseph's Coat, or Amish Bars, with these simple quilted lines and the bright-yellow backing.

TOP: My uncle Donald Riley Duryea with the tenor saxophone and clarinet, circa 1950.
OPPOSITE: Photographed at the Bloch Cancer Survivors Park near the Texas Medical Center, Houston

ODE TO MRS. HOLLY

BLOCK PATTERN: Crazy quilt style

QUILT BLOCKS: Circa 1880–1920. Edge-turned appliqué, hand-basted on muslin.

PURCHASED: American Quilt Study Group, September 2023. $110.00.

FABRIC: Cotton & muslin

BATTING: Warm & Plush 100% cotton

QUILTING THREAD: Superior Kimono Silk 100 wt.

BACKING: Pieced. Free Spirit William Morris reproduction prints.

DIMENSIONS: 80 × 60 in. (203 × 152 cm)

How'd You Quilt That?

These blocks were so impeccably pieced that I was immediately drawn to them. I also love the muted color palette and the variety of prints. Each block was in pristine condition, and professionally prepared. The edges of each appliqué piece were turned under, and the shapes were in the style of Crazy quilts. Crazy quilts are normally made with unusual fabrics—velvets, ribbons, etc.—but these were all cotton prints basted to a thick muslin background.

The dealer labeled the set of blocks "Victorian-era." There are several prints with Japanese iconography, which would fit the Victorian craze for all things Japanese during that era. There are also old prints with French provincial and toile "country" scenes. The mix of these genres is just fantastic, especially since the color palette is so beautifully contained.

Embroidery to the Rescue

When I looked at these blocks, they just called out for embroidery! I decided to embroider them on my Bernina domestic sewing machine, which has thousands of embroidery stitches that I rarely use. For these blocks, I chose 12 wt. cotton thread, which really gives it that look of embroidery floss. I enjoyed stitching these on the machine, and I love the way the thick cotton thread looks.

Vintage Ric Rac Is a Must

I debated on how to piece the blocks together and considered adding a sashing, but I worried that a new fabric might interfere with the style. Since these are pieced in a Crazy quilt style, I decided that butting them up against each other was the best option. However, I felt it needed a little embellishment, so I searched online for cotton ric rac. It was surprisingly hard to find because everything is made with polyester these days. I eventually found 50+ yards of red, vintage cotton ric rac from a vendor at the International Quilt Festival.

For the quilting, I kept it simple, with long, wavy lines across the whole quilt. I didn't want to interfere with the patches or the embroidery, and I like how the wavy lines add some gentle movement. The backing is pieced from William Morris reproduction fabrics, which, of course, fit the time frame of when these blocks were likely constructed.

MRS. HOLLY was not part of my family, but I remember her and treasure my memories with her as if she were a grandmother or aunt. She lived next door to us in La Porte, Texas, in a home on Galveston Bay where we lived for two years.

Mrs. Holly had one son, Sam, and my brother, Eric, and I played with him a lot—always outside, of course; there wasn't much entertainment inside. But I in fact did find something to do inside. After school let out, I would sit inside with Mrs. Holly and listen intently as she taught me how to embroider. I fell in love with embroidery, and I have her to thank.

I still remember her lessons on how to separate embroidery floss, how to use a needle threader, and my favorite lesson—how to make French knots. I loved the small hoops she gave me, and I always felt special when she was teaching me. After second grade, we moved, and I lost track of Mrs. Holly and Sam. I like to think of her when I am stitching these days, especially when I do embroidery.

ABOVE: This quilt was purchased as a set of individual blocks. Each patchwork piece was expertly edge-turned and basted to a thick muslin backing.

A charming old secret garden door at Havenly Farm, Fulshear, Texas.

GRACE'S PINK DRUNKARD'S PATH

BLOCK PATTERN: Drunkard's Path. Brackman #1459.

QUILT PATTERN: Love Ring.

QUILT TOP: Date unknown. Hand-pieced. Bubblegum-pink solids were popular during the 1920s and '30s. It could have also been made as late as the 1970s.

PURCHASED: Gift from Amy Gurghigian. Garage sale purchase, Michigan, circa 2005. About $5.00.

FABRIC: Bubblegum-pink cotton, off-white muslin

BATTING: Warm & Natural 100% cotton

QUILTING THREAD: Aurifil cotton 40 wt.

BACKING: Wide backing. Kaffe Fassett black/white large circle print in cotton sateen.

DIMENSIONS: 67 × 80 in. (170 × 203 cm)

Photographed in downtown Brenham, Texas.

How'd You Quilt That?

Fear, Exhaustion, and Finally Finished

When I was gifted this quilt top, I felt that the simple, repetitive pattern, and the choice of just two solid fabric colors, was not all that interesting on its own. So, I chose to use this opportunity to stitch a whole-cloth motif.

To create the design, I placed the top on my worktable and used painter's tape to mark large sections. I used the seams lines as guides. Within each marked-off section, I created an entirely new, stitched pattern that did not correspond to the patchwork underneath.

There are quite a few imperfections in the lines of each motif I stitched, and I totally embrace them. I went through quite a few emotions while working on this one. At first, I thought the quilting design was brilliant, and I really loved what I was doing. Then, after a week or so, I started to doubt the whole design. I think part of my hesitation is because of the imperfections in my stitching. Because we have become so accustomed to seeing technical precision in computer-aided quilting motifs, I felt my free-motion motif was really lacking on this ambitious whole-cloth design.

It took some time, but I eventually chose to embrace my work along with its imperfections. This need for perfection is something that holds us back, especially women. And it is not easy to let go of this habit. With this quilt, going through all these emotions and learning to let go frankly left me exhausted. I feared I would lose the motivation to finish. I even took this quilt off the longarm machine and started on another quilt. I hung it on the design wall and let it sit. After a few weeks, as I eyed it from time to time, I started to like it again. When I finished the other quilt, I loaded this one back on the longarm and went back to work.

I'm now at peace with the imperfections, and I'm really happy with the way it turned out. From afar, this accomplishes exactly what I intended—an interesting, stitched motif in black thread over a timeless patchwork pattern.

MYRTLE GRACE DURYEA HAUSHAHN was my paternal grandfather's sister, and she was the oldest of Elva and Amelia Duryea's eight children. Grace was born in 1888 and died in 1961. She was born on homesteaded land in Richardson County, Nebraska. Later, she went to work in her father's general store in Nims City.

Myrtle Grace loved to sing and play the piano. She and Archie Bacon had two children, born in 1917 and 1920, and then a third child was born in 1930. After Archie died, she moved to an apartment in Falls City and, later, to Kansas.

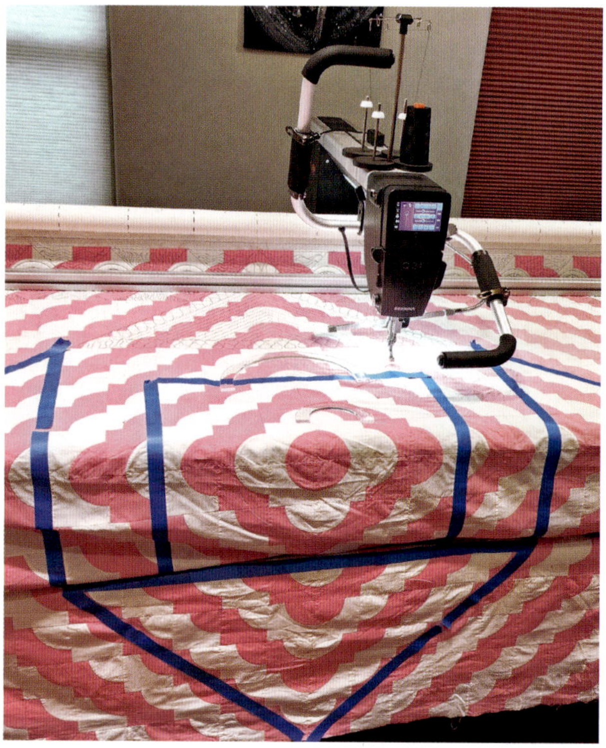

ABOVE: This progress photo of the quilt loaded on my longarm sewing machine shows how I used painter's tape to mark off each section before quilting. This tape does not leave residue. Next, I created a stitched motif within each section, using rulers and free motion.

OPPOSITE: Photographed in downtown Brenham, Texas.

WHAT'S IN A NAME? ESPECIALLY THE DRUNKARD'S PATH

This quilt top was given to me by Amy Gurghigian. She purchased it at a garage sale circa 2005, and it sat in her closet for almost two decades. The Drunkard's Path block is my all-time favorite name for a quilt pattern. The backstory of this name is both funny and fascinating. It is believed that the name was actually created around the turn of the nineteenth century as a way to raise awareness of the dangers of "drunkenly men" and to support the temperance movement. Quilt researchers have also written about how, historically, some women did not like to spend time stitching a block with such a scandalous name. So, it's been renamed over and over, which I find hilarious.

Many quilters know this pattern by different names, such as Solomon's Path, Old Maid's Puzzle, Mill Wheel, Wanderer in the Wilderness, and Rob Peter to Pay Paul. But it is the curious Drunkard's Path name that is the most popular. When I posted this quilt on Instagram, I learned that a Drunkard's Path block formed in a concentric pattern like this quilt is called a Love Ring.

AMELIA & HER UNFORGETTABLE OCEAN WAVES

BLOCK PATTERN: Ocean Wave. Brackman #2628.

QUILT TOP: Circa 1880–1900. Hand-pieced.

PURCHASED: eBay, March 2023. $290.00.

FABRIC: Cotton

BATTING: Warm & Natural 100% cotton

QUILTING THREAD: Aurifil cotton 50 wt.

BACKING: Pieced. Vintage, uncut cotton sacking material, Notan Brand rice, pieced with solid cotton borders. The rice sack material was gifted to me circa 2010.

DIMENSIONS: ±50 × 75 in. (±127 × 191 cm)

How'd You Quilt That?

Modern over Classic

I love this top. It is small, but the colors are striking. It is a great example of a classic Ocean Waves pattern. There are thirty-nine blocks, each one measuring about 5 inches. The original edges of the quilt were left unfinished in octagon shapes, so I left them alone and attached the binding by following those lines.

I chose to quilt a ¼-inch grid over the whole quilt, using a 50 wt. cotton thread. The modern grid over this classic pattern creates texture, but when you study the quilt from afar, the grid seems to fade away, and your eye can focus on the patchwork.

To create this grid, I first stitched from left to right across the entire quilt, using the longarm frame channel lock feature, which allows the machine to travel along the rails while creating perfectly straight lines. If you are stitching on a domestic sit-down machine, you can get the same straight lines by using the foot as a guide or trying a seam attachment guide. If you are using a longarm that does not have locks for straight lines, you can use a ruler. Just be careful to keep each section straight.

After I covered the entire quilt with horizontal lines, I took the quilt off the frame, turned it 90 degrees, and reloaded it on the machine. I stitched the second set of lines by using the same process, from left to right.

Repairs

The quilt top was in good shape, except for the middle block, which did not lie flat. The center muslin patch had stretched out and was wavy. I removed the muslin fabric, flattened it, and reattached it to lie flat. I typically look for quilts that don't need a lot of repair, because this can be tedious. But if the repairs are limited to one small area, they are worth it.

TIP: For a grid like this, always quilt in the same direction. It seems easier to stitch from left to right and then, when you get to the end, just travel back in the opposite direction, but I do not recommend this. Always stitch from one side to the other and repeat the exact same direction for the next line. A back-and-forth motion will create puckers. Stitching in only one direction will achieve the smoothest stitches possible.

AMELIA ROSE BACON DURYEA was my great-grandmother (mother of Crip). Her parents, Elmer and Sarah Bacon, moved to Richardson County, Nebraska (after living in Pennsylvania) sometime after the end of the Civil War. Elmer and four of his brothers served in the Civil War as part of the Pennsylvania regiments. It is highly possible that the family lived in, or near, the small town of Duryea, Pennsylvania.

Amelia married Elva Duryea in 1887, and they had eight children. Elva was elected Richardson County commissioner in 1915. He also worked as a blacksmith, and he owned a general store in Nims City. He owned one of the first four cars in Richardson County and later opened a car repair business, where my grandfather Crip worked.

Not as much is known about Amelia, but I am certain she sewed, cooked, cleaned, cared for her children and husband, and most likely made a lot of quilts for her family. She was most likely born sometime around the end of the Civil War. The first of her eight children was born in 1888.

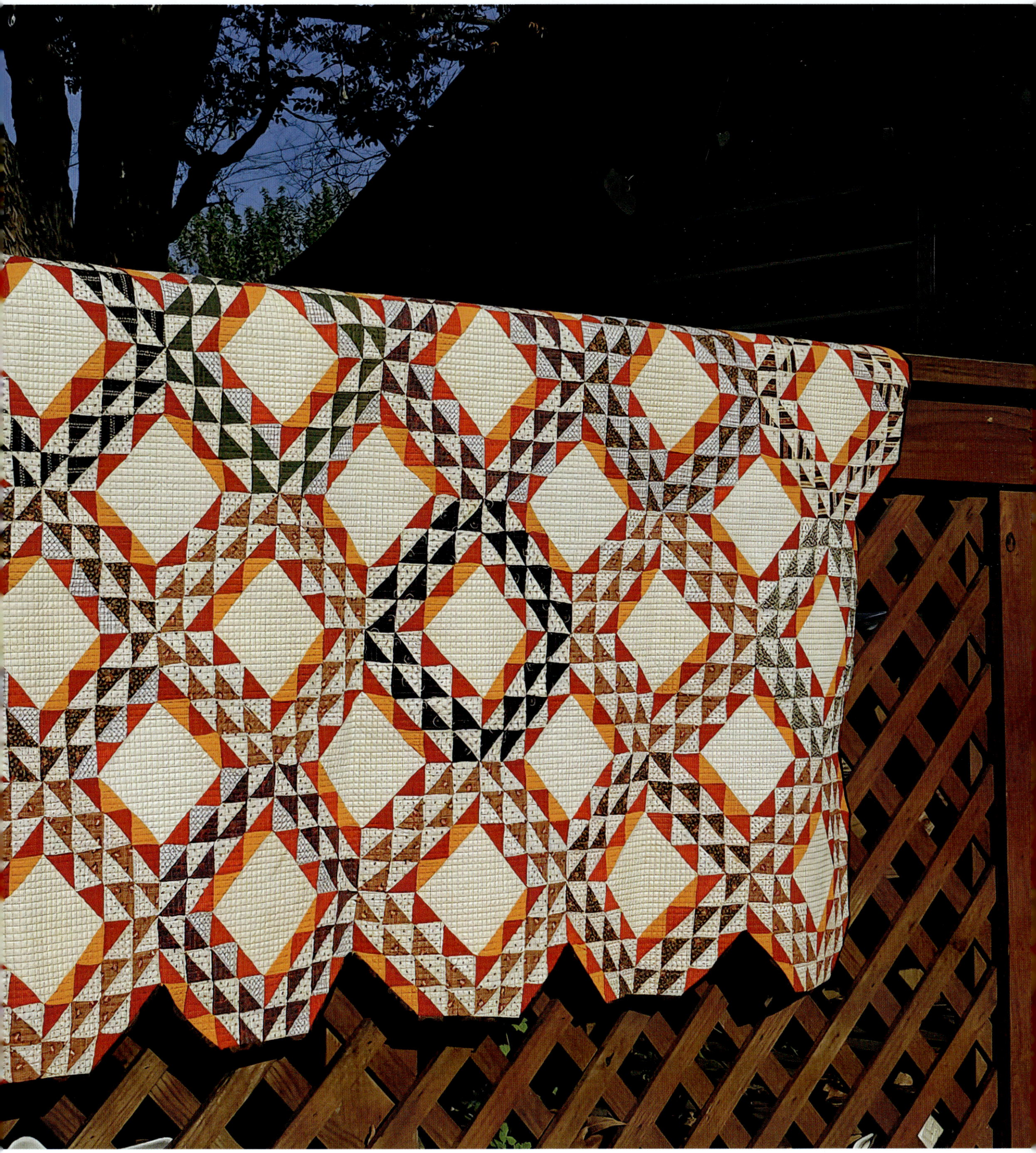

CIRCLES & BERRIES FOR UNCLE PAUL

BLOCK PATTERN: Original design with appliqué circles, vines, and tulips; stuffed berries.
QUILT TOP: Circa 1850s, according to dealer
PURCHASED: Antique dealer, September 2023. $650.00.
FABRIC: Cotton & muslin
BATTING: Warm & White 100% cotton
QUILTING THREAD: Aurifil cotton 50 wt.
BACKING: Pieced. Yuwa Japanese cotton print.
DIMENSIONS: 86 × 94 in. (218 × 239 cm)

OPPOSITE: The creek in Wimberley, Texas, is a serene setting for this very old quilt.
Photo by Jimmy Wong.

How'd You Quilt That?

Don't Smash the Berries!

These stuffed berries were part of the original quilt. Quilting them on a longarm frame, where the finished three layers are rolled up on a take-up bar, was a bit of a challenge.

At first, I was hesitant to put this top on the longarm because of the stuffed berries on this very old quilt. I worried they would get smashed as the quilt was rolled up on the take-up bar—I literally worried all night about those berries. They were the centerpiece of this quilt, and I didn't want to ruin them. So, I did two things. First, I was extremely careful when rolling the quilt as I stitched it. And second, I decided to work very long hours so I could remove the quilt from the longarm frame as soon as possible. I finished stitching this top in just two days.

Those Muslin Inner Borders Are Too Big

The background fabric of this top is muslin. I felt that the large borders between the blocks were plain and empty, which meant they were an open canvas for me to fill with pattern. I chose to fill those in with repeating circles stitched in red and yellow thread.

The outline for each circle was created with an acrylic ruler, in order to make perfect circles. I created two different designs to use inside the circles. For the vertical sashing, I filled the circles with a ¼-inch matchstick grid, using a straight ruler. In the horizontal sashing, I combined a ribbon pattern with matchstick lines in the center.

Free-Motion Circles and Tulips

All the quilting (except the circle outlines) is hand-guided, free-motion. The red star centers are densely quilted, and I stitched motifs on top of the appliqué. The space outside the appliqué is stitched, using a flame motif. This is a simple back-and-forth motion and is a nice filler. When you make a sharp point at the beginning and end of each "flame," it creates a striking design.

My uncle Cecil Paul Duryea Jr., me, and my aunt Polly Duryea photographed at St. Mary's Cemetery in Dawson, Nebraska, in 2013. Photo by Jimmy Wong.

I'VE NAMED THIS QUILT after my uncle Paul Duryea. He was so much like my dad that it was a bit eerie. We used to say they were identical twins separated by ten years. Their voices, their movements, their looks, and even their extroverted personalities were almost identical.

Cecil Paul Duryea Jr. was born in 1925 and passed away in 2017. Paul was career military and served in the Air Force. He and my Aunt Polly were married for sixty-eight years. After he retired, Paul and Polly moved their family to Humboldt, Nebraska. My brother and I spent many summers at their home, along with all my cousins and my grandparents, who lived in the next town over. Paul was a strict taskmaster, and he often put my brother and me to work on the family farm.

Paul appreciated art, and I think he would have loved to have seen this quilt and know that it has been named in his honor. He and my Aunt Polly were a big part of my life, especially during my teenage years, and I have always treasured my relationship with them.

A HIPPIE LOG CABIN FRANCES WOULD LOVE

BLOCK PATTERN: Log Cabin. Brackman #2573.

QUILT TOP: Circa 1950–1970. Hand-pieced.

PURCHASED: Gift from Amy Gurghigian. Garage sale purchase, Michigan, circa 2015. About $5.00.

FABRIC: Various cotton commercial prints, pieced

BATTING: Warm & Natural 100% cotton

QUILTING THREAD: Aurifil cotton 50 wt.

BACKING: Pieced. Commercial cotton prints in various sizes.

DIMENSIONS: 74 × 83 in. (188 × 211 cm)

How'd You Quilt That?

Staying Simple

This Log Cabin, just like the Barn Raising quilt, called for a super-simple quilting motif. I chose to create organic straight lines (no ruler) in yellow and orange cotton thread.

Here's Why Washing Is Problematic

This is one of the reasons why experts don't recommend washing quilt tops in a washing machine. This one shredded a lot, but it held together. Older quilts might not survive.

Amy purchased this quilt top at a garage sale in Michigan around 2015. She gifted the top to me. But while she owned it, she washed the quilt top, which was probably effective in eliminating any smell, but it made a huge rat's nest of thread on the back. I cut tons of loose threads before quilting it.

I NAMED THIS improv Log Cabin after my paternal grandmother, Frances, because these are fabrics that she would have used in her lifetime. If she wasn't cooking, cleaning, tending her garden, or raising her chickens, Frances was at her sewing machine. She wasn't a prolific quiltmaker, but she did make a few. She loved sewing clothes, dolls, doll clothes, and everything else. She even made beautiful appliqué banners for St. Mary's Catholic Church in her hometown of Dawson, Nebraska.

When I was little, half of my wardrobe was made by Frances, the other half by my mom. Frances also made tons of impeccably sewn Barbie clothes and other doll clothes. My grandfather Crip even built wooden Barbie doll beds for my cousin Anne and me. Then Frances sewed us tiny mattresses for those beds!

Sewing Clothes for My Sister and Me

The fabrics in this quilt remind me of my own early days of learning to sew, especially the red-and-white gingham. I have very vivid memories of sitting at the kitchen table in our house in Katy, Texas, making tops for my sister and me from red/white gingham fabric.

ABOVE: My grandmother Frances Irene Riley Duryea, pictured with the parish priest working on a patchwork quilt at the St. Mary's Catholic Church hall in Dawson, Nebraska, early 1970s. Photos were special back then, so even though the quality of this image is poor, the fact that it exists is priceless.

OPPOSITE: Photographed in downtown Brenham, Texas.

RED & BLACK FOR SMOKEY

BLOCK PATTERN: Drunkard's Path / Love Ring. Brackman #1469 & #1470.

QUILT TOP: Unknown date. Dealer suggests 1930s and attributes this top to Amish makers. Machine-pieced and hand-pieced.

PURCHASED: eBay, April 2025. $287.50.

FABRIC: Cotton

BATTING: Hobbs Tuscany 100% Wool

QUILTING THREAD: Aurifil 40 wt. cotton

BACKING: Wide backing. White-on-white cotton print.

DIMENSIONS: 75 × 81 in. (191 × 206 cm)

How'd You Quilt That?

This strong red-and-black pattern demanded a quilting motif that didn't detract from these graphic forms. I chose to match the thread color to the fabric and opted for 40 wt. cotton thread because it is a bit thicker and would add texture to the shapes. Each time I changed the top thread, I also changed the bobbin thread. So, the backing design looks impressive on the lightly colored backing fabric.

Once again, I turned to two of my favorite repetitive motifs—the flame and bubbles. Each section of black patches was quilted with a flame motif. The red sections were quilted with bubbles. Doing so made finishing this quilt a true joy. I didn't have to worry about creating a new motif for each section. Rather, my plan was set, and all I had to do was follow this simple idea to finish the whole quilt.

For this quilt, I chose a wool batting because I wanted to get some extra loft. Wool is perfect for adding a little umph, and that's why it is often a favorite choice for art quilts and quilts that have special techniques.

I found this quilt top on eBay, and I was riveted by this bold design and these strong colors. The dealer touted this quilt as Amish. I don't have any proof of this, but it is highly possible. It is a classic pattern that was meticulously stitched. Regardless of who the maker was, it is a stunning quilt top with great colors, and I am thrilled that it is now finished.

MAN, I LOVED THAT HORSE. We spent hours and hours together during my preteen and teenage years, and we knew each other better than some humans can know each other. This is not a great photo; Smokey is fitted with only his halter, not a bridle, which means I wasn't riding him, just sitting on him. But of course, back in those days we didn't take photos every minute—so I treasure this one.

I did own a nice Western saddle, but I rarely used it. It was heavy and the leather always seemed to pinch my bare skin, because yes, I often wore shorts while riding my horse. Jeans were just too hot for this Texas kid. Mostly I just jumped on bareback, and we took off, and yes, I was mostly barefoot too. And no sunscreen either!

Smokey started out as part of the Harris County sheriff's mounted patrol, so he was very calm around cars and other city noises. When he retired, he came to live with me. I was in seventh grade at the time and had been riding horses with my friends since second grade. I always wanted my own horse, and I was incredibly lucky that my parents, who knew nothing about caring for horses, took the plunge and trusted me to care for him.

Smokey's fur was pitch black, so the vivid red-and-black quilt seemed appropriate to name after him.

ERIC'S ROOM

BLOCK PATTERN: Checkerboard or One Patch.

QUILT TOP: Unknown date. Hand-pieced.

PURCHASED: American Quilt Study Group, September 2023. $100.00.

FABRIC: Cotton

BATTING: Warm & Natural 100% cotton

QUILTING THREAD: Aurifil cotton 50 wt.

BACKING: Pieced. American Made Brand solids and other cotton prints.

DIMENSIONS: 79 × 69 in. (201 × 175 cm)

How'd You Quilt That?

A simple pattern called for simple quilting. I quilted inside of each patch as a way to honor the patchwork and keep the top's design intact.

Each red block is stitched in close, organic (no ruler) matchstick lines. The off-white patches were created with a variation of the ribbon motif. The blue patches are filled with the flame motif.

Old tops in this pattern have that iconic checkerboard design that is so timeless. By quilting within each patch, there is no visual interference with the overall design.

From left, **me; my little sister, Pauline; and my brother, Eric. This photo was taken in the 1970s, in front of our house in La Porte, Texas.**

GROWING UP, we kids rode our bikes to school every day. Eric had a cool three-speed bike with a banana seat that was all his own. I was given my mom's bike, with a toddler seat on the back.

Throughout my elementary school years, each morning while my parents were at work, I would make breakfast for myself and my sister and brother. Then I would get myself ready for school and my toddler sister, Pauline, ready for daycare. I put her on my bike and dropped her off at daycare, then went on to Bayshore Elementary. And like Ginger Rogers, who danced backward and in heels, I did all that wearing a dress! Dresses were the required dress code in those days (even for public school), and for the record, it was a dress code I despised.

Our house was a modest two-story, with three small bedrooms upstairs. My mom decorated each of our rooms. Mine was very girly, with a fancy bedspread with pastel flowers and matching curtains. Eric's room was red, white, and blue. When I saw this quilt top, it immediately reminded me of that room and the days our family spent in that house.

The red and blue patches have certainly faded over time, but I felt that this top was worth saving and would be fun to quilt. Each time I look at this quilt, I'm reminded of my brother, Eric, and also of my mother and her flare for interior design. Eric and I were close in age, Irish twins as we were often called, and he passed away way too early, in 2017.

A THOUSAND PYRAMIDS FOR MARY BETH'S COUCH

BLOCK PATTERN: Thousand Pyramid. Brackman #111a.

QUILT TOP: Circa 1890s. Hand-pieced.

PURCHASED: eBay, August 2023. $220.00.

FABRIC: Cotton

BATTING: Warm & Natural 100% cotton

QUILTING THREAD: Aurifil cotton 50 wt.

BACKING: Wide backing. Kaffe Fassett cotton sateen print with large flower vases.

SIZE: 76 × 85 in. (193 × 216 cm)

This old Ford pickup makes a charming backdrop for this classic patchwork pattern. Photographed at Havenly Farm, Fulshear, Texas.

How'd You Quilt That?

An Odd Attraction

While flipping through eBay one evening, I came across this quilt top and I loved the fabric choices, especially the print of the girl, or doll face. That one triangle is pieced into this quilt perfectly and really adds personality to the design. In fact, it was that one triangle and all its charm that enticed me to buy this old quilt top.

The top was in excellent condition, but one corner was not finished, so I left it as is. You can clearly see the missing row of triangles, and these little nuances are all part of the charm of an old quilt top.

A Design for Each Patch

One of the most effective ways to finish an old quilt without masking its design is to quilt one small motif within each bit of fabric, or within each block. Keeping the motif contained is more cohesive than a big overall design that does not coordinate with the patchwork. I turn to this method over and over again, studying each patch, or series of patches or block, and choose a free-motion design that fits that particular fabric and shape.

Choosing a thread color is the fun part. With blocks that are busy prints, I typically chose a thread color that blends in with the colors of the fabric. However, if you want contrast, or to highlight your quilting, you can choose a color that stands out.

MY MOM, Mary Elizabeth Lennemann Duryea (1937–2023), or Mary Beth as she was known, loved to decorate, and she was good at it. I think if she were still with us, and if I were to offer her a choice of all my antique quilts, she would choose this one and drape it over her couch in her Prince Street house in Houston's Heights neighborhood. The colors and vibe would fit her decorating style perfectly, so I named this one after her.

My mother, Mary Elizabeth Lennemann Duryea, 1955.

DOC'S WINDOW

QUILT PATTERN: Broken Star. Brackman #4007.5.

QUILT TOP: Unknown date

PURCHASED: Antique dealer, September 2023. $150.00.

FABRIC: Cotton

BATTING: Warm & Natural 100% cotton

QUILTING THREAD: Aurifil 50 wt. cotton

MACHINE EMBROIDERY: Aurifil 12 wt. cotton thread

BACKING: Pieced. Commercial print in a vintage reproduction design.

SIZE: 72 × 83 in. (183 × 211 cm)

How'd You Quilt That?

The quilt maker drew circular feather motifs in a dark pencil in each of the negative-space blocks. Along the side blocks, she drew a half-circle feather motif. It would be nearly impossible to try to remove the pencil marks, so I opted to keep them and to machine-stitch over them in a thick cotton thread. I did this on my domestic machine, not the longarm, because I felt it would be easier to control the quilting along these pencil marks. Because the feather motifs are stitched in 12 wt. cotton thread, the finished look resembles hand embroidery.

Each of the diamonds in the star designs is quilted with its own motif in a matching thread color. The machine-stitched feather motifs are quilted with matchstick quilting in orange thread.

There is a bubblegum-pink inner border, and, initially, I considered removing it. The pink doesn't match the colors of the diamond patchwork. But ultimately, I left it in place because that's the way the maker assembled it. I quilted it in a ribbon motif in navy-blue thread, in order to diffuse a bit of the bright pink.

Overall, with the matchstick lines over the machine-stitched feathers, and the dense quilting in the patchwork, this quilt looks so elegantly finished. Even though the date when this quilt top was made is unknown, I can easily picture it back in the 1930s, draped on a bed in a gorgeous old home filled with antique furniture.

This photo shows the machine embroidery I stitched over the pencil lines, before it was quilted on the longarm.

MY MATERNAL GRANDPARENTS, Doc and Marie Lennemann, operated a medical office together in Falls City, Nebraska, starting sometime in the 1920s and continuing through the late 1950s. Their office in downtown Falls City sat right on the main town square, across from the Richardson County Courthouse.

After they retired, the window from the exterior door of Doc's office (that he shared with a lawyer) was removed, and someone had the brilliant idea to save the window. The windowpane was framed, and it hung in my parents' house for years. Eventually I took possession of it, and it now hangs in my home, directly above the antique desk from Doc's home office.

Doc would often treat patients at his home in the off-hours, or, as was common back then, he also made a lot of house calls. He needed both a downtown and a home office, and the desk I now use was once Doc's home office desk. My dad also used this same desk when I was growing up. Sitting at this old desk and writing books, articles, and lectures, and looking at that heavy framed glass with its white crackling lettering, makes my modern home feel a little homier.

This Broken Star quilt seems fitting to the time in which Doc lived and worked, and I can picture it draped over his couch or folded at the foot of their bed.

ABOVE: Dr. Ernest Lennemann, my maternal grandfather.

OPPOSITE: The colorful walls and retro signage at one of my favorite restaurants on Washington Ave. in Houston formed a perfect backdrop for this Broken Star quilt. Photo by Jimmy Wong.

JOE WAH'S FEED SACKS

BLOCK PATTERN: Half-square triangles in variations of Brackman #2785 Mosaic #11, or #2124 Mosaic #12.

QUILT TOP: Circa 1930s–1940s

PURCHASED: eBay, August 2023. $151.55.

FABRIC: Cotton

BATTING: Warm & Natural 100% cotton

QUILTING THREAD: Aurifil 50 wt. cotton

BACKING: Wide backing. Commercial cotton print with vivid turquoise and red colors.

DIMENSIONS: 67 × 69 in. (170 × 175 cm)

A barn beautiful enough for a chandelier is a welcoming backdrop for this colorful quilt. Photographed at Havenly Farm, Fulshear, Texas.

How'd You Quilt That?

The vivid colors in this top are really special. I loved the choice of this light-blue (or aqua?) fabric in the negative spaces. The light-blue blocks are quilted with a simple flower motif in matching thread. Each mosaic block with the half-square triangles is quilted with a ribbon motif in a matching thread color.

The quilting choices for this quilt proved once again that a simple plan to quilt within the patches is a wonderful way to honor the patchwork and complete the design. In addition, once you make the decision to quilt the first mosaic block and the surrounding negative-space blocks, there are no more decisions to make for the rest of the quilt other than thread color. So, it becomes a fulfilling process to stitch ribbon and flowers over the entire top.

As you stitch on old quilt like this, it allows you time to reflect on all these quirky feed sack fabrics and enjoy the tiny elephants, the mandolins, and the flowers that once held a variety of dry goods such as flour, sugar, coffee, and grains.

MY MOTHER-IN-LAW, was born in a tiny village in China, not too far from Guangzhou. She was born in 1911, immigrated to the US in 1955, and spent her first few years here living in Mississippi. One year after she arrived, at the very old age of forty-five (not so old now, but rare back in those days), she gave birth to a son, my husband, Jimmy Wong.

These very American feed sack fabrics are a fitting reminder of her, because she was a very frugal and practical woman. I'm sure when she set up her new life here in America, she would have saved and reused all the cotton sacking she could find. In fact, she and my father-in-law owned a small country grocery store in Greenwood, Mississippi, and another one later in Houston, so she would have had access to plenty of dry goods stored in cloth bags.

Joe Wah was a wonderful mother-in-law. She was never fluent in English, and she never learned to drive. But she knew enough English to speak bits of it to me, and I learned a few words and phrases in her dialect of Cantonese. Interestingly, she would speak to me in English only if no one was around. The minute my husband or anyone else walked into the room, she would switch to Cantonese. Another funny language story is that my Chinese pronunciation was so awful that she often had no idea I was even trying to speak to her in Chinese.

I called her Nyen Nyen, which is the baby talk version of the name for the paternal grandmother, Nyen. Chinese language has different names for the paternal and maternal grandparents. Such a great idea—you know immediately where the grandparents fit in with the family without having to ask. Clearly, she was not my grandmother, but it just seemed to work out that I would call her by the same name that my children called her.

Nyen Nyen helped care for our two children when they were infants and through their toddler years while my husband and I worked. Later in life, she spent her last five years living with us in our suburban Houston home.

She was passionate about gardening, a skill that was born out of necessity from living in a small Chinese village during a very difficult era. If you didn't grow food, you didn't eat. She always had a thriving garden, and even into her nineties, she would traipse outside several times a day to plant, weed, and harvest.

Joe Wah was never fond of dogs, and we had a 90-pound dog in those days named Chip. Occasionally, rabbits would discover her beautiful garden, and they were a huge nuisance. One day Chip caught and killed one of those rabbits. That big black dog became her best friend after that! Needless to say, we ate a lot of fresh vegetables thanks to her. All of us truly miss that garden and her. Joe Wah passed away at the age of ninety-five in 2008.

LEFT: My mother-in-law, Joe Wah, circa 1950s.

MIDDLE: My in-laws holding their first baby to be born in the US, and the baby who later became my husband, Jimmy Wong.

RIGHT: Photographed in Brenham, Texas.

MOM'S FOLK ART APPLIQUÉ

BLOCK PATTERN: Original design with Princess Feather variation. Appliqué.

QUILT TOP: Unknown date (probably late twentieth century).

PURCHASED: eBay, $225

FABRIC: Cotton

BATTING: Hobbs Tuscany 100% Wool

QUILTING THREAD: Aurifil 40 wt.

BACKING: Wide backing. Free Spirit William Morris reproduction print.

DIMENSIONS: 74 × 76 in. (188 × 193 cm)

A red barn, a deep-blue sky, and a gorgeous quilts slung over the fence—a picture-perfect setting at Havenly Farm, Fulshear, Texas.

How'd You Quilt That?

It's impossible to know when this quilt was made, but I don't think it is that old. My best guess would be the 1980s or somewhere around there. After quilting so many old tops with muslin, I really appreciated the nice white cotton background. These classic colors on a bright-white background make this appliqué so vivid and fun.

The folk-art shapes are large and uncluttered, which makes them the perfect canvas to add stitching. I stitched the bubble motif inside each of the large red flowerpots. Along the diagonal sawtooth sashing, I quilted matchstick lines in the red triangles and left the white triangles unquilted.

For the center section, I quilted straight lines ¼ inch apart in a thicker red thread. Normally I would not quilt over an appliqué design like this one, but I felt that the straight lines would add texture and structure over the design without detracting. The lines were created with a ruler for the shorter lines at the top and bottom of the on-point square. The longer lines across the middle were stitched using the frame channel locks on my longarm.

TIP: For long lines like these, or ones that go across an entire quilt, if you are working on a noncomputerized longarm machine like I am, when you advance the quilt and roll it up on the take-up bar, the quilt can shift. Sometimes one-half of the quilt can be slightly higher or lower after you move it. It is a textile, after all. So, before you begin stitching a new set of matchstick lines, test where the stitched lines will fall, and make sure the distance between the lines is equal. If not, you can gently tug a little bit on one side of the quilt to line it up, or you can add a scrap of batting behind the take-up bar to raise one side a slight bit.

IF THERE HAD BEEN an empty wall in my mom's house, she would have hung this quilt there. These vivid red and green and yellow fabrics pop off that white background, and this folk-art imagery is an aesthetic she would have loved.

When I was growing up, my parents moved every two years or so. We were not a military family, and we didn't move for my parents' work. The reasoning for all that is a long story. Anyway, after I graduated from high school, my parents lived in one house for the next thirty years. It was a 1950s one-story, with one bathroom, in Houston's Heights neighborhood, surrounded by beautiful old trees. This quilt would have fit my mom's vibe beautifully.

TOP: My mother, Mary Elizabeth Duryea, had a flair for interior decorating. Photo circa 1950s.

RIGHT: Photographed at Havenly Farm, Fulshear, Texas

BRENHAM FIRE COMPANY
No. 1

MRS. WILSON'S FIRST GRADE CLASS

BLOCK PATTERN: Schoolhouse. Brackman #865.

QUILT TOP: Unknown date. Hand-pieced.

PURCHASED: Xenia Cord's Legacy Quilts. International Quilt Festival, Houston, 2024. $275.00.

FABRIC: Cotton. Original colors were red, yellow, green, brown, and blue. All are slightly faded. The blue has almost completely faded to a gray/brown color.

BATTING: Warm & Natural 100% cotton

QUILTING THREAD: Aurifil cotton 40 wt.

BACKING: Pieced. Kaffe Fassett cotton print with retro flowers on red background.

DIMENSIONS: 80 × 60 in. (203 × 152 cm)

How'd You Quilt That?

"Etch A Sketch" Fun

My first thought for this top was to stitch minimalist lines and preserve the graphic boldness and simplicity of these faded schoolhouse blocks. But then I had a second idea. Go big and have fun! I sat down with paper and pencil and sketched out a few childlike drawings for practice. I decided to start stitching at one end of the border/sashing and not stop till I got to the other side. This eliminated all the thread issues with starting and stopping, and that made this quilting infinitely more enjoyable. Each small motif is an original drawing that I created on the fly. The overall effect is definitely maximalist, but I feel that I added something new to this top that is all my own, and kind of unforgettable.

SCHOOL BUS
SCHOOL BUS

MRS. WILSON was my first-grade teacher. She was the only Black teacher in an all-white public elementary school. Mrs. Wilson certainly had courage. She was also a fierce teacher, and the students respected her. We have all been shaped by the teachers in our lives. They come into our life briefly, then we both move on. Over time, some are more memorable than others, and the lessons they taught us are priceless. I don't know where you are, Mrs. Wilson, but I remember you and I thank you. This quilt honors you and your career as a wonderful teacher.

SCHOOL BUS
SCHOOL BUS

BRENHAM

COMPANY

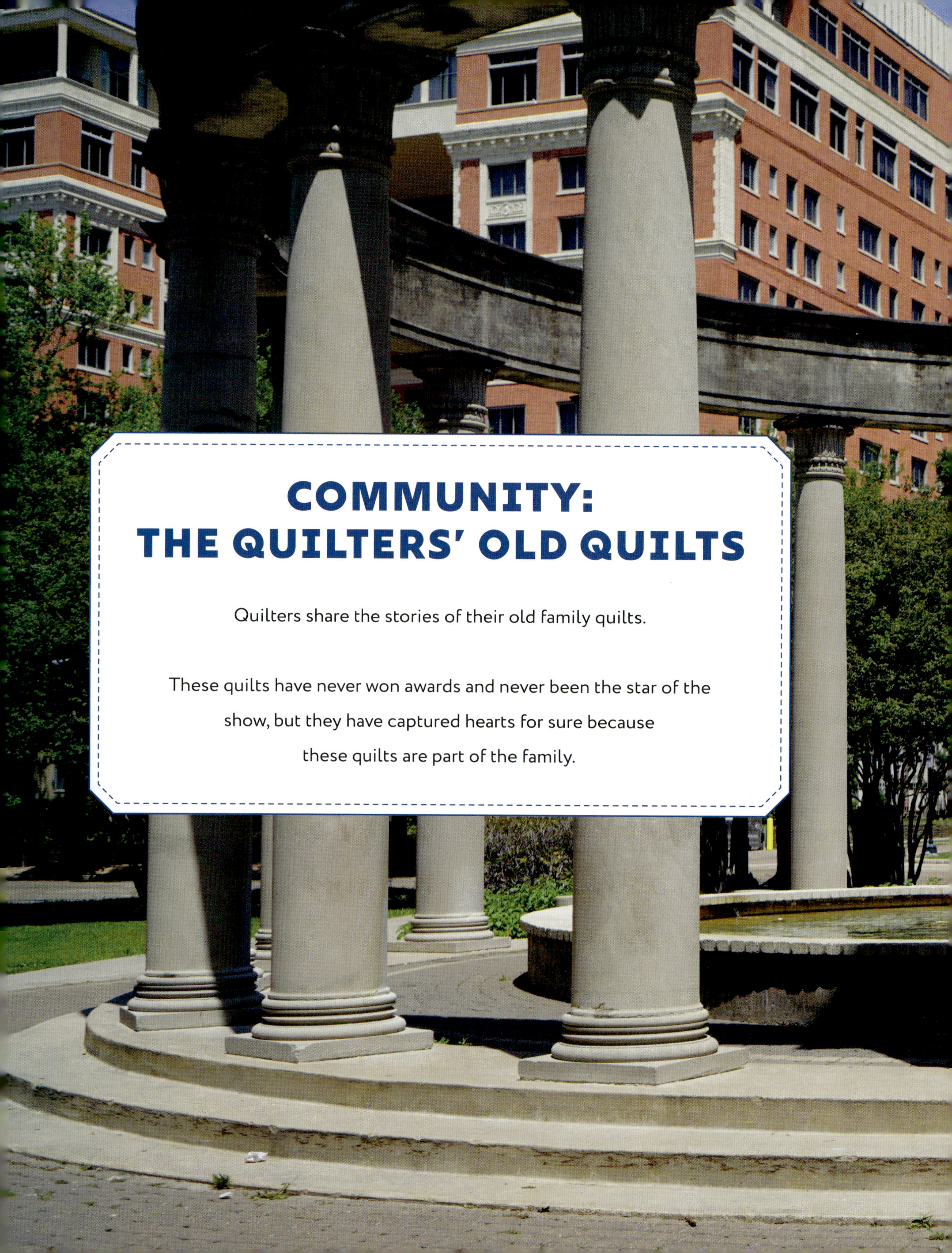

COMMUNITY: THE QUILTERS' OLD QUILTS

Quilters share the stories of their old family quilts.

These quilts have never won awards and never been the star of the show, but they have captured hearts for sure because these quilts are part of the family.

These bright colors on this old quilt pop in Houston's museum district.

FRANCES & PEARLS' FOREVER GIFTS

By Teresa Duryea Wong
Houston, Texas

My paternal grandmother, Frances Irene (Riley) Duryea, had a tiny sewing room at the top of the stairs in their small home. I can still picture her sitting there at her machine, sewing something amazing. She was an incredible doll maker and dressmaker, and occasionally she made quilts, two of which I own. I also have one quilt in my collection made by her mother, Pearl (Riley) Bacon, which appears to have been made later in her life. These quilts are a part of my past, made by the hands of my ancestors. A forever gift.

The author wrapped in a quilt made by her grandmother.
Photo by Jimmy Wong.

Now, allow me to share some precious family quilts from a few wonderful quilt people. You may have seen an award-winning quilt from one of these contributors, or maybe you've taken one of their classes. You might have snapped a photo of one of their quilts at an exhibition, or perhaps you've seen them featured in magazines showcasing their stunning talents. But here's something you haven't seen: an exclusive peek at one of the quilts they love the most. These quilts have never won awards and never been the star of the show, but they have captured hearts for sure because these quilts are part of the family.

RIGHT: Pearl Bacon Riley—my great-grandmother—made this quilt, most likely in the 1950s. It is an interesting design for its time and the layers are tied, rather than quilted. This treasure has been used and loved by her family for years. Photographed in Houston, Texas, by Jimmy Wong.

BELOW: This quilt was made by my paternal grandmother, Frances Riley Duryea, circa 1960s. Photographed on the land bridge over Memorial Drive in Houston, with the downtown skyline in the distance. Photo by Jimmy Wong.

A MOTHER-DAUGHTER COMBO

By David Owen Hastings

Sequim, Washington

My mom, Marian Bickford Hastings, was a big fan of the early American decorating style. She grew up in a colonial farmhouse, which is now a small historical museum in Vermont. When my parents relocated to Iowa in the late 1950s, Mom brought her love of New England to our small rural town. She filled our home with family antiques from New England, plus a few things purchased at the local Ethan Allen furniture store.

At some point in the late 1960s, my mother purchased a quilt kit. She most likely bought it from our local Hancock's Fabrics, or from Amana Colonies, a nearby German enclave. I'm not sure about this, but I'm guessing that Mom bought the kit because of its design, which was a perfect fit for the style of our house. But it was my maternal grandmother, Harriet Bickford, who made that quilt as a gift for my mom. I vaguely remember my grandma working on it when she would visit us in Iowa. She lived in Vermont, where my parents were born.

David Owen Hastings is a modern quilter and popular teacher. He lives in Sequim, Washington. Photo by Azuree Holloway for *Quiltfolk* magazine.

My grandmother hand-stitched this kit quilt as a present for my mom. The date on the quilt is July 27, 1970, my mom's birthday, and I believe that's when it was finished. I was seven years old at the time. While I'm sure my grandmother wanted to give her daughter a nice gift, she probably also knew that my mom was too busy raising five kids to have time to finish the quilt on her own.

ABOVE: Harriet Bickford lived in Vermont and often came to visit her daughter and five grandchildren in Iowa.

OPPOSITE: David's maternal grandmother, Harriet Bickford, made this family quilt as a gift for his mom, who was busy raising five kids. It was finished in July 1970.

OPPOSITE: This quilt was made from a 1960s kit that features a cross-stitch design and is hand-quilted.

RIGHT: David Owen Hastings's childhood home in Iowa in 1966.

During a visit to the Pacific Northwest Quilt & Fiber Arts Museum one day, I was surprised to walk in and see that same quilt on the wall. I learned that the quilt my parents had on their bed for as long as I can remember is known as a Cross-Stitch Quilt. The quilt on display at the museum was also made in Iowa, so clearly this was a popular design in that region. I think the white fabric was originally printed with cross-stitch patterns in a water-soluble ink, which is completely gone. I'm sure this quilt was washed countless times. At some point, I believe my sister Pamela wrote the label information on the back of our family quilt, probably using a Sharpie, since that's what we had back in 1970.

This quilt is in great shape, considering it was used daily for at least two decades. The hand-stitched crosses and hand quilting look pretty fresh, even today. It's lovely to look at all that hand stitching and hand quilting. Every time I see this quilt, I think of my grandma, who was a stern New Englander but also very gentle. She is the one who taught me to how sew on our home sewing machine, a Singer Rocketeer, around the same time she was working on this quilt. I've been stitching with that same sewing machine for over fifty years now.

RIGHT: The label was handwritten in Sharpie, which is not ideal, but at least the details of the quilt are permanently recorded.

AUNT HELEN'S WEDDING GIFT

By Terrie Hancock Mangat

Taos, New Mexico

When I got married in 1970, my aunt Helen Saalfeld Rymarquis gifted me a quilt that she had hand-quilted and hand-appliquéd. It was such a beautiful wedding gift, and I've carried on that tradition by making my own nieces and nephews and other family members quilts for special occasions.

My cousin Sally, Helen's youngest daughter, was my age, and we went to high school together. Sally's older siblings were already out of the nest, so she and I spent a lot of time together and had many sleepovers. When we were at her house, Sally and I loved going into the attic and rummaging through all the stuff that was shoved up there after years of raising a big family.

This is a silkscreen print that Terrie made of her mom's family when she took a printmaking class in college. Her aunt, the quiltmaker Helen Saalfeld Rymarquis, is seated on the far right. Her mom, Esther Saalfeld Hancock, is seated, second from left.

ABOVE: Terrie Hancock Mangat is an art quilter whose innovative, embellished artworks were instrumental in establishing the art quilt movement in the 1980s. She continues to create striking and highly original quilts from her home in Taos, New Mexico. Her quilts are in countless private collections and museums and have been exhibited widely. Photo by Azuree Holloway for *Quiltfolk* magazine.

OPPOSITE: Helen Saalfeld Rymarquis's quilt hanging in Terrie Hancock Mangat's Taos, New Mexico, home

Helen Saalfeld Rymarquis made this quilt as a wedding gift for her niece, Terrie Hancock Mangat, in 1970.
Photograph by Barry Norris Studio.

My mom, Esther Saalfeld Hancock, did not sew, but Aunt Helen was always stitching something. She loved creating hand embroidery and working on hand-appliquéd quilts. She had a favorite chair where she sat to stitch. I too have a favorite leather chair where I sit to create my reverse hand appliqué and embroidery. I often think of the parallels of our hand stitching, and sewing was something I always shared with both Helen and Sally.

Digging this quilt out of my storage for this book brought up a lot of memories of Helen and those years I watched her sew. What's more, when I look at this quilt now, I realize exactly how precise my aunt's stitching was. It was really perfect.

Terrie and her husband, Dick Kinkade, dance alongside Terrie's quilt *Dancing* (2008). Photo by Azuree Holloway for *Quiltfolk* magazine.

MY GREAT-GREAT-GRANDMOTHER'S *CHICKASAW STAR* QUILT

By Emma Alcazar

Powhatan, Virginia

I am the sixth firstborn daughter in a long line of firstborn Chickasaw women. My great-great-grandmother Minnie Keel Liddell, a Chickasaw woman born in the 1890s, overcame incredible obstacles in her life, including winning an Oklahoma Supreme Court battle in 1936 to save our family land.

Quilt making has been a part of my family for generations. From the time she was a young girl, my grandmother Linda vividly remembers watching her own grandmother fold and cut fabrics for quilting. Minnie made this quilt for my grandmother Linda Dean Briggs in 1975. As a tiny girl, I remember seeing this quilt on a bed in my grandmother's house.

When I began my own quilting journey, my memories of this quilt were always in the back of my mind, connecting me to my family's artistry and strength. To my knowledge, it is the only one of Minnie's quilts that have survived through the years.

The Lone Star quilt that my family fondly calls a *Chickasaw Star* is hand-pieced and hand-quilted. My grandmother Linda had the foresight to embroider Minnie's name and date in one corner, ensuring that her work wouldn't fall into anonymity. My grandmother gifted it to me in the early 2020s, and I cherish this gift of love that reaches down through the years, connecting our family!

ABOVE: Emma Alcazar (*right*) is pictured with her grandmother Linda Dean Briggs. Emma is part of a long line of quilt makers who began her own quilt-making journey in 2001. She creates art quilts that reflect her Chickasaw heritage. Emma's quilt *Iláyya'sha Katihma (We Are Still Here)* is part of the permanent collection at the International Quilt Museum.

OPPOSITE: This *Chickasaw Star* quilt is the only known surviving quilt made by Minnie Keel Liddell, an enrolled citizen of the Chickasaw Nation. Her granddaughter Linda Dean Briggs had the foresight to label it with her name and the date, 1975.

LEFT: Minnie Keel Liddell (*left*) was born in the 1890s. She is pictured with Linda Dean Briggs in a photo from 1977. They are the great-great-grandmother and grandmother to Emma Alcazar. Both women, and Emma as well, are part of a long line of Native American artists.

OPPOSITE: Emma Alcazar is now the proud owner of this quilt made by her great-great-grandmother in 1975. Emma comes from a multigenerational family of Chickasaw artists.

LEFT: Emma Alcazar is keeping her Chickasaw heritage alive by learning her Native language. She is also following in the footsteps of the women in her family by making quilts to give away. Emma made this Chickasaw alphabet quilt to give away to a new mother.

1975

A BABY QUILT FOR HEIDI

By Heidi Parkes

Milwaukee, Wisconsin

Before I was born in Chicago, Illinois, in 1982, my maternal grandma, Mimi (Marion Montgomery), organized a collaborative family quilt to commemorate my birth. I remember at around age four receiving an artist's sketchbook from Mimi and posing for sculptures and drawings in our family room while she was a student at Peck School of the Arts at the University of Wisconsin–Milwaukee.

Mimi later lived in Santa Fe, New Mexico, where we would open her kiln to discover how the "Kiln Gods" had transformed our pottery. She instilled in me a lifelong trait of staying curious and open to the unfolding process of art making.

Initially, this quilt was hung on the wall in my bedroom, and when I was five, it was relocated to the foot of my bed, where I began to recognize that the makers were beloved people in my life. Through sewing this quilt, they cast a collective and heartfelt spell to remind me of the support of my extended family, filled with wishes welcoming me to life.

Mimi incorporated her passion for the alphabet (her favorite game was Scrabble), and she inspired my great-grandma Meta Nickles to add a "C" for Cat too. Mimi gave everyone a white fabric base to create their block and was surprised by the fact that two blocks completely disregarded her base! But, like her *Jack Be Nimble* block implies, she nimbly found a way to balance them at the base of the quilt.

Heidi Parkes is a fiber artist whose hand-stitched and hand-embellished works are wildly popular among modern quilters. Her quilts often incorporate secondhand materials, and they showcase her immense talent in the art of mending. Heidi is also a teacher, and her work has been shown in dozens of exhibitions. Photo by Jeff Parkes

Heidi Parkes can feel the love of the women in her family in this quilt they jointly made when she was born in 1982. It was created by Kitty Hieb, Linda Erickson Hill, Rose Loth, Marion Montgomery, Becky Moosbrugger, Lori Neal, Betty Nickles, Gulrose Nickles, Meta Nickles, Linda Emard Parkes, Rosemary Parkes, Patti Sonnenberg, Sylvia Sula, and Barb Waters. Marion, Heidi's grandmother, organized the construction of the blocks and provided each maker a blank white fabric base. Most followed instructions, but two makers disregarded her plain white base and contributed their own original blocks, seen here on the bottom row.

I'm aware of Mimi completing four quilts: my baby quilt, a "big sister" quilt for me when my brother Jeff was born in 1985, and bed quilts for herself and my mom. Incomplete for decades was a puff quilt that I finished for Jeff's 2014 wedding, and never to be was a quilt-as-you-go for my Aunt Becky.

Mimi purchased a hand-pieced Log Cabin quilt top at an estate sale for $37.50, and in 2013, I turned that top into my first-ever hand-quilted quilt. The experience sparked my career as a quilter within a year.

Heidi's mom, Holly Parkes (*left*), is pictured with her mother, Marion Montgomery, holding the quilt the women in their family made for Heidi's birth.

Detail from the baby quilt made for Heidi Parkes. This block was made—and signed—by Heidi's maternal grandmother, Marion Montgomery.

A WILD QUILT MADE BY STELLA, MAYBE

By Erin Suliak

Yellowknife, Northwest Territories, Canada

The quilt has my grandmother's name in marker in the bottom corner, written there when Stella Staples went into a dementia care facility. When I brought it to a family reunion ten years after she had passed, no one recognized the quilt. Like many of our family quilts, though, my mother and aunts could tell stories about familiar fabrics they recognized, although the construction was a curiosity.

ABOVE: Erin Suliak is a multidisciplinary artist who performs and works in both textile art and sculpture. Her creative modern quilts often include recycled materials, as well as hand-dyed fabrics. Erin also is a spinner and embellishes her fiber art with felting or embroidery. Draped over her is a family quilt possibly made by her grandmother Stella Staples. Erin lives in Yellowknife, Northwest Territories, Canada, where she was born and raised.

RIGHT: Erin Suliak describes this quilt as a bag rag laid flat. Yet, this wonky assemblage of color and shapes is a quilt she truly treasures, and it continues to inspire Erin in her own art practice.

No one in my family can confidently identify who made this quilt, and several think it was created by Stella, who had an indifferent attitude to quilting. The construction is unorthodox, and the stitching haphazard, which my mother thinks appropriate to her mother's style.

My great-grandmother Pearl Staples and great-aunt Gladys Sellars were a quilt-making machine for a large extended family. Every birth or wedding was cause to create a quilt. For grandchildren and great-grandchildren, they would appliqué bright double-knit polyester fabrics into shapes. Alphabet letters, tulips, animals—mine is a yellow dog quilt that I treasure. Each pup features a monochromatic set of fabrics, and they're blanket-stitched and hand-quilted. I enjoyed visiting my cousins to compare their quilts to mine, familiar forms and crazy colors.

This quilt, which I claimed after my grandmother Stella died, is not like any of those quilts. It features pieced elements interspersed with laid appliqué elements and is tied with a variety of yarns. It looks like a rag bag laid flat. Fabrics seem to have been used as found, no trimming, just spontaneous explosions of color and shape. Some bar elements dissolve into unordered patches here; a couple of fan elements are squished together there. I can discern three columns, but it is hard to read because the appliqué is rowdy and clusters in unusual ways.

I love this wild thing and draw inspiration from it in my art practice. I've come to view this quilt as a metaphor of Stella's mind as she traveled further and further into dementia. Some elements have a semblance of order, others fractured and dissolving into disconnected array. It is beautiful, it is weird, and perhaps it is less important that we know who made it than to know it is loved.

ABOVE: Stella Staples is possibly the maker of a wildly creative quilt that is now owned and loved by her granddaughter, Erin Suliak.

OPPOSITE: These detail images reveal the chaos and creativity of this unusual quilt. It is believed to have been made during the 1970s.

TATTERED PARTS TO HANG ON THE WALL

By Kelly Spell
Hixson, Kentucky

I made this piece by using a small section of a family quilt that was passed down to me from my grandma Bonnie Slater. The exact origin of the quilt is unknown, but it's possible that Bonnie inherited it from her mother, Marjorie Gladys Dennis Hess, or from one of her grandmothers, Etta Carolina Dennis or Mollie L. Hess.

When I received the quilt, the majority of it was tattered and no longer usable. In 2018, I decided to cut out small sections that were in okay condition and embroider them. The embroidery was both decorative and functional—it secured pieces of torn cloth and gave me a way to stitch my own story into the quilt. I found it surprisingly

Kelly Spell is a bold modern quilter whose quilts exude a colorful, abstract aesthetic. Her pieced quilts are exquisitely constructed and tightly quilted, and she often returns to variations on the circle as her signature shape. Kelly's quilts have won numerous awards and have been exhibited at Quiltcon and Quilt National, as well as other venues and museums. She lives and works in Hixson, Tennessee. Photo by Audrey Esarey.

When Kelly Spell was given an old family quilt, it was tattered and worn. But she found several sections that were worth saving. She cut them out and embroidered through the three layers. Adding the embroidery was a way to incorporate her own story into this beloved textile, and it helped reinforce the frayed fabrics. She mounted these small, quilted sections onto artist canvas and gifted them to her family and kept one for herself.

difficult to push the needle through the tightly woven fabrics, despite their wear and tear. Perhaps that is a testament to the strength of generational bonds.

I mounted several sections of this quilt onto artist's canvases and gifted them to my family members. Several years passed before I got around to making one for myself. Isn't that always the case? Now it hangs in my studio, a small but constant testament to the quilters who came before me.

BELOW: This priceless photo shows not only Kelly Spell with her grandmother Bonnie Slater, but also one of the first quilts Kelly ever made back in 2016. Kelly made this quilt as a gift for Bonnie and the photo was taken at Bonnie's home in The Villages, Florida.

SURPRISE! MY GREAT-GRANDMOTHER WAS A QUILTER

By Tara Miller

Atlanta, Georgia

When I began quilting at age forty, I thought I was the only person in several generations of my father's family who made quilts. I'd never seen a quilt made by anyone on his side of the family. No one talked about quilts. No one used homemade quilts. The word *quilts* wasn't part of the family lexicon.

Then one day, a couple of years after I started quilting, my dad arrived at my house with a surprise—a quilt made by Grandma Bartlett, my great-grandmother.

Frances Carrie Chappell Cook Bartlett (1904–1969) died four years before I was born, but she was mentioned often by family who remembered her. She made this quilt in the 1940s from printed and plain feed sacks and coarse cotton yardage—materials that reflect what she and Grandpa Bartlett sold in the rural, dirt-road grocery store they owned from 1937 to 1956 in Heafer, Arkansas.

LEFT: Tara Miller is a traditional quilt maker who teaches, lectures, and is a pattern designer and a historian. Her research and lectures connect the power of women's history and the art of quilt making to remind us of our rich and diverse heritage. Tara is a former producer for a video program in partnership with the International Quilt Museum, and the producer of the *Six Know It Alls* show. She is a past member of the Board of Directors of the American Quilt Study Group. Tara lives in Atlanta, Georgia, and she is seen here hugging the only known quilt made by her great-grandmother. Photo by Azuree Holloway for *Quiltfolk* magazine.

OPPOSITE: This 1940s quilt was made by Frances Carrie Chappell Cook Bartlett. Her great-granddaughter Tara Miller especially appreciates its intentional design in the face of such scarcity of time and materials.

It's the only quilt made by her that any of us know still exists. Even so, my attachment to it is more than sentimental. Grandma Bartlett's quilt embodies two things I talk about often in my antique-quilt lectures: intentional design in the face of scarcity—or even because of it, and intentional design within a utilitarian context.

She took time to contemplate an overall layout. Her use of the two constants: Red on the vertical and green on the horizontal gives order to the chaos. The repeated red and green strips organize what otherwise seems to be completely random. This deliberated design shows us that this quilt was more than a thing to keep a body warm. It was a fragment of her mind and spirit. A piece of her.

Now, what about that one end where the colors are reversed? I think she laid the quilt out on the bed and saw that it was a bit too wide and not quite long enough, so she whacked a column off one side and slapped it on the end. Practical. Done. A quilt that fit the bed.

Seems this quilting thing is in my DNA, after all.

TOP: Tara Miller's great-grandparents owned a country store during the 1930s in a tiny town in Arkansas. Tara is the elated owner of the only known surviving quilt made by her great-grandmother.

ABOVE: Frances Carrie Chappell Cook Bartlett made at least one quilt in her lifetime, and it now belongs to her great-granddaughter Tara Miller.

OPPOSITE: Tara Miller, a quilt historian, instructor, and maker, says the red and green bars create an artistic structure in this 1940s quilt made by her great-grandmother.

LOVED TO PIECES: A QUILT BY AUNT JOAN

By Deborah Fisher
Long Island, New York

My husband's Aunt Joanie was a quilter, sewer, knitter, and spinner. She did it all, and she could talk about it all day to anyone who would listen.

Joan Cash was self-taught. One of the very first quilts she made was a wedding quilt for us in 1995 with blocks in the Bear Claw pattern. The background and backing were unbleached muslin, and it was envelope style, with no binding. This quilt has been used so much over the years by both my husband and me, as well as our two children, that today it looks like a giant rag. A supersoft, well-loved, made-with-joy rag that is full of memories and comfort.

After that wedding quilt, Joan made dozens of other quilts as gifts for her nieces and nephews and their spouses, great-nieces and -nephews, and even her great-greats. We have a pile of her quilts and unfinished quilt tops that will be eventually given to family in the future, continuing to share her love with the family she never got to meet.

When Joan died, I was honored to have the task of dispersing her collection of materials and tools into the world, daunting as it was. Along with yarn, roving, and an array of other fiber supplies, she had a vast and diverse fabric collection ranging from Civil War reproductions to blue-and-white Japanese fabrics to colorful, modern fabric prints. I inherited her Juki sewing machine that she loved so much.

Joan always talked about being buried with one of her quilts. So, when she died, we chose a colorful Irish Chain quilt to bury her with. Not one of her most accomplished quilts, but we felt it was just right for her: the Irish Chain for her heritage, the cheerful colors, and a symbol of her always persevering and learning new things.

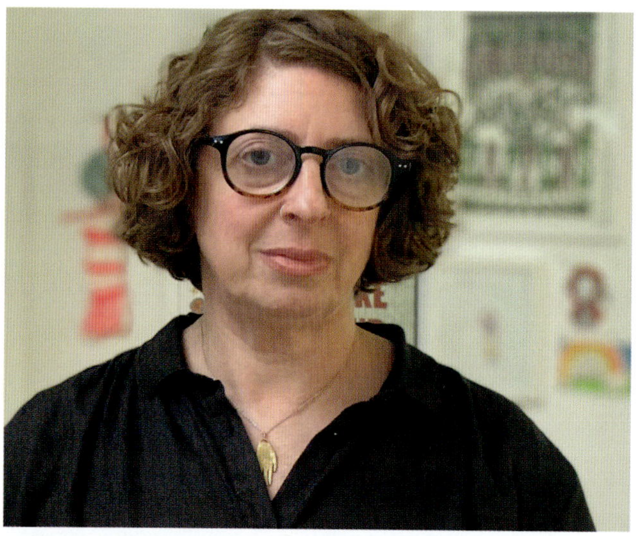

LEFT: Deborah Fisher is the owner and founder, and self-described ringleader, of a creative handmade business known as Fish Museum & Circus. She is a fabric designer and the beloved creator of quirky ceramic pincushions that are so popular among quilters that when the doors open at the Modern Quilt Guild's annual Quiltcon event, quilters run—superfast—directly to her booth to line up to buy one. When Deb is not busy designing or curating her curiosities, she also makes quilts. She lives on the north shore of Long Island, New York. Photo by Andrew Cash.

ABOVE: Joan Cash was a prolific quilter, spinner, knitter, and sewist. She was also the aunt of Deborah Fisher's husband, Andrew Cash. Joan is pictured here with her great-niece Hazel Cash in a photo from 2005.

OPPOSITE: This quilt has been loved almost to pieces. It was made by Joan Cash as a gift for Deborah Fisher and her husband, Andrew Cash, when the two got married in 1995.

GRANNY MILDRED'S TIMELESS *TRAIL OF TEARS* QUILT

By Teresa Duryea Wong

Bixby & Marble City / Cherokee Nation, Oklahoma

Excerpt of an article originally published in* Quiltfolk *Magazine 31: Oklahoma. Reprinted with permission.

"All of us grandkids have one of Granny's quilts. Some of us have more quilts than others," Casi Morris said with a grin. One of the most prized quilts in Casi's possession is a timeless, original design created and handmade by her grandmother Mildred Choate Taylor, or "Granny," as Casi calls her.

While Mildred has been quilting on and off for most of her eighty-plus years, Casi is relatively new to quilting. Mildred and her children and grandchildren are enrolled citizens of the Cherokee Nation. Mildred lives in Marble City, Oklahoma, and Casi lives in Bixby, Oklahoma. The "Granny quilt" that Casi cherishes most is titled the *Cherokee Removal Quilt* (2019), also known as the *Trail of Tears*.

The design features alternating long rows of diamond patchwork, colorful prints, and solid white. "When the Cherokee were forced to move, many of them had already switched to Western ways and were wearing denim and gingham, so the colorful strips represent their clothes," Mildred explained.

LEFT: Casi Morris is a quilter, but the most cherished quilt she owns is one her "Granny" made that depicts the forced removal of Cherokee off their natural lands. Casi and her grandmother Mildred Choate Taylor are enrolled citizens of the Cherokee Nation and live in Oklahoma. Photo by Azuree Holloway for *Quiltfolk* magazine.

OPPOSITE: This quilt is titled *Cherokee Removal Quilt* (a.k.a. Trail of Tears). It was made in 2019 by Mildred Choate Taylor and quickly snatched up by her granddaughter Casi Morris. Photo by Azuree Holloway for *Quiltfolk* magazine.

Interspersed between the colorful patches are several different hues representing the myriads of skin tones for the people whose lives were intertwined with the Cherokee's. For example, Mildred used tan to represent mixed ethnicities of Indigenous and white. White strips are meant to represent the missionaries. And the black strips represent the enslaved individuals held by the Cherokee people.

"The diamond patches in the quilt represent the tears, and these are set in black, which is meant to represent death," Mildred added. In addition, the long rows of solid white represent snow along the trail.

"I have a deep appreciation for history, and I love Granny's *Trail of Tears* quilt so much," Casi said. "Granny has served on the national Trail of Tears board for most of my life, and she attends conferences every other year. Some of my fondest memories of growing up are going with Granny on car trips to those conferences. For me, as one of four kids, having all that one-on-one time with Granny was a dream. So even though the event itself was a horrible tragedy, I have really sweet memories attached to those trips, and especially Granny and this quilt."

Mildred's *Cherokee Removal Quilt* is just one of many quilts she has crafted in her lifetime, but this one is special because it is her own interpretation of the painful past of her ancestors. By choosing to capture this story through a quilt, she has chosen an art form that can be held, and loved, and can even keep Granny's descendants warm for years to come.

LEFT: Mildred Choate Taylor has been quilting on and off for most of her eighty-plus years. She's pictured here sitting on a bench in Marble City, Oklahoma. The town dedicated this bench in her honor on her eightieth birthday, in recognition of her volunteer and civic contributions.

RIGHT: Mildred Choate Taylor, an enrolled citizen of the Cherokee Nation, explained that these diamond patches are set in black to represent death that happened during the Trail of Tears when Cherokee were forced off their land. The diamonds themselves represent the tears of her ancestors. Photo by Azuree Holloway for *Quiltfolk* magazine.

A BRIT'S TREASURED AMERICAN STAR QUILT

By Sarah Hibbert
London, England

TOP: Sarah Hibbert's mom, Jenny Overton, loved knitting, and her father, Frank Overton, loved art.

LEFT: British graphic designer Frank Overton bought an American quilt in Colorado in the 1970s that his teenage daughter, Sarah Hibbert, quickly claimed for herself. That quilt later inspired Sarah to take up quilting.

I grew up in a house full of color, design, and creativity. My father, Frank Overton, was a graphic designer who collaborated with various companies designing and rebranding their corporate images. I was the youngest of three children and came along once my father's design practice was already established. Therefore, I was extremely fortunate to be the one dragged to endless book shops and art galleries from an incredibly early age, while leaving my mother at home to continue her love of knitting. So, there was no sewing in our house!

ABOVE: Sarah Hibbert is a modern quilter, author, patternmaker, and teacher based in the UK, with a vibrant personality who always has a funny story to share. From her studio just outside London, Sarah transforms timeless quilt designs into fresh contemporary art quilts. She's known for her love of linen and for her beautiful hand-stitching. She's a very busy quilter and world traveler who teaches and travels pretty much everywhere there are quilts, even as far away as South Korea.

This quilt has an epic story. It is not a family quilt like others have shared on these pages, but, once it entered Sarah's home, it quickly became family. Her parents purchased the quilt during a trip to Colorado in the 1970s and brought it back to their London home. Sarah latched on to the quilt, and it sat at the foot of her bed for years. Later, this beloved American souvenir even inspired her to take up quilting.

Our home was a clutter of objects ranging from beautiful paintings to ceramics, tin toys, and decoy ducks. Every item was equally important to my father. My brothers and I were brought up to live life with eyes wide open.

In the late 1970s, my parents used to attend the Aspen Design Conference in the USA, meeting up with the likes of Charles and Ray Eames, Saul Bass, and other movers and shakers of the design world. They always returned home with treasures and stories from their visits.

During one extended visit, they were taken to a vintage market in Boulder, Colorado, and while there my father was very much taken with a quilt showing a star design made with nine large blocks, all using the basis of a half-square triangle. The quilt measures 100 by 100 inches.

It consists of various plain and print fabrics, and I am presuming these are dress scraps rather than fabric bought specifically for the job. The quilting is quite a simple floral design in the main squares and crosshatched across the borders. The batting is a fine cotton, quite worn away and thinning in places. Unfortunately, there is no date or signature on the piece. I am still unsure how they transported it home, since their bags were always so full of folk art and books.

This quilt was my first introduction to quilting. It was around my late teens, and I was very conscious of fashion and having the right design look for my bedroom. My furniture was very modern and of the time, and even though the quilt was old and a little frayed, it somehow made the room feel warm and comforting. From the moment the quilt came into our home, I claimed it for myself. It was mine and not going anywhere else! It sat proudly on my bed and became my comfort blanket during my teenage years and early courtship. When it came to the time for me to move out and start my married life, this was top of my list to take with me into my new home. It has remained on or near my bed and is still holding together despite many years of love and attention.

In 1986, when I was a new mum, I took myself off to an evening class to learn quilting, totally inspired by visions of the star quilt in my bedroom. After those first lessons, I was hooked! The quilt gave me a love of textiles before I was ready to discover the joy of quilting. I have on various occasions set out to re-create it properly, but somehow I never quite get started. Probably because the quilt is one of my most treasured processions and kick-started my interest and love of quilts. So much so that I do not want to share that feeling with a new-generation piece.

THIS QUILT TALKS!

By Linda Pumphrey

Bella Vista, Arkansas

I am a humble, crazy quilt, a favorite quilt of the person who owns me. I do not have wonderful, rich, jewel-tone silks and velvets, but cotton calicos of mostly pastel colors. I am not highly embellished but machine-stitched, adding to my simple and unpretentious appearance.

My makers were a recognized artist and an award-winning quilter. I live in a closet of handmade and elegantly stitched quilts created by both individuals. Several of these quilts have ribbons they won hanging in shows. These award-winning quilts have beautiful fabric bought to make them. For me, they used left-over cotton fabric from dresses and aprons. From these discarded pieces of cloth, my block shapes are random. One could say the shapes are crazy with a degree of free spirit.

I was not placed on the bed for display or admiration. My purpose was to keep the child lying underneath me warm and safe on cold nights. When she was little, she would look at my fabric and find prints of the dresses and aprons she had seen her mother and grandmother wear.

Why am I a favorite? It's because I hold a piece of her mother's dress that she remembers from childhood. It is

Linda Pumphrey finally retired after working for Mountain Mist for several decades. When her coworkers asked her why she stayed so long, even through multiple buyouts, she told them she stayed for the quilts. Today, Linda is a renowned expert on Mountain Mist patterns and has published a book on the topic. She is a passionate collector of vintage and antique quilts made of small pieces and has also written a book on red-and-white quilts. The International Quilt Museum is also fortunate to be the recipient of Linda's tireless support over the years.

not like the rest; this fabric stands out a little because it is not pastel but gray and red. Just like this piece of fabric, my owner was taught by her mother and grandmother not to be flashy, that it's okay to be a little crazy, to be a free spirit, and to stand out just a little.

TOP LEFT & LEFT: Linda's mother, Marvy Vesta (Gieseker) Pumphrey, and her grandmother Mida Vesta (Summers) Gieseker combined their talents to make a simple, utilitarian quilt for Linda when she was a child.

ABOVE: Mother-daughter duo Marvy Vesta (Gieseker) Pumphrey and Mida Vesta (Summers) Gieseker were accomplished artists and award-winning quilt makers. They typically purchased special fabrics specifically for intricately designed quilts. But for this family quilt, they used scraps from family garments. Today, it is a favorite quilt among hundreds of quilts owned by Linda Pumphrey.

JIM THARPE: THE HARTSFIELD AFRICAN AMERICAN SLAVE QUILTS' LAST CARETAKER

Seattle, Washington

By Teresa Duryea Wong

Excerpt of an article originally published in* Quiltfolk *Magazine 32: Washington. Reprinted with permission.

Jim Tharpe's grandmother Lena Caldwell Hartsfield learned to quilt as a young girl, and she was taught by her grandmother Miss Molly, who was born an enslaved person in Tennessee around 1840. Miss Molly believed that quilts could keep a family history alive. She had the fortitude and courage to hold on to some of her quilts, including a large, Checkerboard quilt she made in the early 1850s, while she was still enslaved. It's believed she was thirteen years old at the time, and Jim has that very quilt in his collection.

This extremely rare quilt, along with eleven others, is part of the Hartsfield African American Slave Quilts Collection, which has been passed down through Jim's family. In addition to the Checkerboard, there are four other quilts made by Miss Molly before she was emancipated, and seven made by other women in Jim's family dating from the late 1800s up to the 1960s.

RIGHT: Jim Tharpe is the last caretaker of a collection of family quilts that includes a quilt by his great-great-grandmother made before the Civil War. He is pictured at the Columbia Gorge Museum in front of a quilt made for him by his aunt Eureda Jones, called *Wedding Quilt* (circa 1960s).

OPPOSITE: Miss Molly, as she was known, was the great-great-grandmother of Jim Tharpe. She made this quilt (known as the *Checkerboard Patchwork Quilt*) as a teenager before the Civil War, circa 1855. She was taken from her family as a young child and enslaved. She kept this quilt in her possession and was able to pass it down to her family, which Jim says is a "slice of American Black history rare among today's Black families."

"I am the last caretaker of these quilts," Jim said. "My quilts represent a slice of American Black history rare among today's Black families. It is an honor to be the keeper of these family quilts, but at the same time, it is an issue I have to deal with. They are getting old and need care and preservation."

Jim wants these quilts to be seen. He'd love for them to travel to every state in America. Ultimately, he wants to find a permanent home for the collection, but he doesn't want them to go in a box and to be seen only once every ten years.

Part of the reason he wants these quilts to be shown is because quilting can teach us a lot about history. Specifically, Black enslaved Americans, including Miss Molly, were denied the opportunity to live with their biological families, and as a result the term "family" takes on an entirely new meaning in African American history.

"These are family quilts. All of the pieces that went into her quilts were meant to represent her family and friends," Jim said. In Miss Molly's case, she was taken from her family as a young child and "given" to the son of a slave owner. So she made her own family with the people who were around her. "There were about a hundred people in the small town of Woodlock, Tennessee, where my great-great-grandmother lived," Jim said. "She considered all of them to be her family."

During the summer of 2024, all twelve quilts in the Hartsfield Collection were on display at the stunning Columbia Gorge Museum, in Stevenson, Washington, which has breathtaking views of the river canyon. "The numbers of people who have come to see these quilts have been amazing," executive director Louise Palermo said. "People looked deeply at these quilts; some even sobbed. What I love about these quilts is this is a family story. What I have in front of me is a validated oral history of a woman who passed down her story with her own mouth to Jim's grandmother, and she also taught that grandmother how to sew."

"For me, it's been pleasant surprise to watch people's reaction to these quilts [at the Columbia Gorge Museum]," Jim said. "It is hard for people to believe that some of these quilts are nearly two hundred years old."

Jim took possession of the collection in 2005, when his mother, Verna Tharpe, passed them down to him. Though they weren't brought out of the storage chest much when he was growing up, the family always told stories about these quilts.

"As an adult, I learned more about the American arts-and-crafts movement and Southern culture and traditions, and that's when I started connecting all the childhood stories I had heard to these quilts. On the oldest quilt, made by Miss Molly before the Civil War, you see bloodstains that are possibly 160 years old. Were they from the whip, rape, childbirth? One can only imagine what life was like," Jim explained. "I obviously never knew my great-great-grandmother, but I feel her presence every time I look at her quilt."

The young boy who's spent a lifetime with quilts in the background now hopes he can protect this precious collection of historic African American quilts. His dream is to preserve these quilts so that future generations will know the story of Miss Molly and all that she endured to survive—and not only that she survived, but that she was an extraordinarily talented quilt maker.

OPPOSITE: This family quilt was made circa 1900 and is known as the *Country Fair* quilt.

FOLLOWING SPREAD: The Hartsfield African American Slave Quilts Collection includes quilts made by eight women in Jim Tharpe's family, starting with his great-great-grandmother who was enslaved before the Civil War.

Crossroads Quilt
As enslaved people made their way north, they relied on many signs to navigate safely. Each square features a plus sign symbol representing a crossroads and careful consideration of each road chosen. The main crossroad was Cleveland, Ohio, where there were many routes to freedom.
Colors play an important role. Green represents love, peace and safety. Red means danger, stay alert. Orange means bounty.

A BIG QUESTION: ADDING VALUE OR DESTROYING VALUE?

This is an age-old question for unfinished antique quilt tops.

The vivid colors in the Joseph's Coat quilt pop against the Mecom Fountain backdrop in Houston, Texas.

My Aunt Polly Duryea and I often share an old-fashioned "bed turning" at her home in Lincoln, Nebraska. A bed turning is a timeless pastime where quilts are placed on a bed and turned one by one to study them. These quilts are part of Polly's antique quilt collection.

One day, I was shopping at the booth of an antique quilt dealer. I found a quilt top I loved and struck up a conversation with the woman working that day. To be fair, I do not know if she was the owner, and I have no knowledge of her expertise in this field. But when I explained that I planned to finish the quilt on a modern longarm sewing machine, she said, "No, you can't." Then she gently pulled the quilt top out of my hands and back toward her. I wanted to argue my case, but instead I just left in frustration. I wondered, was this vendor in the business of selling quilts and quilt tops? Or were they some kind of self-appointed arbitrator of what is acceptable and what is not?

Some experts feel that if you change, or alter, an antique object, you have forever changed its value. Some even go further and say that any alteration destroys its value as an antique. I want to dig a little deeper into that theory and question whether it applies to all quilt tops, or just some of them. And more importantly, what happens to all those "valuable" unfinished antique tops sitting in the bottom of someone's closet?

The experience of cleaning up the homes of loved ones who have passed away is usually difficult. Making decisions about what to do with all the stuff from that person's life is tough, and often emotional. Very few people can keep everything, so hard choices have to be made. And if you have had this experience and you have tried to gift antique china or crystal, antique furniture, and, yes, even antique quilts to young people, you may get the same reaction that millions of millennials and younger generations share—they don't want all that old stuff. Their aesthetic leans modern, and some even seek lives with less stuff.

Again and again, I get calls and emails from people who ask me what to do with their relative's old quilts. Here is

a real example that I am certain is played out repeatedly in homes across the country.

A distant relative of mine passed away. She was a very talented quilter, and she was also a passionate antique-quilt collector with a great eye. Her daughter, Sarah, had memories of going with her mom into Amish communities in the 1980s and '90s and purchasing quilts directly from makers. Now that her mom was gone, Sarah was trying to find a home for all the quilts. The siblings and other relatives took a few of the ones she had made herself, but nobody wanted the antique quilts. Several of these quilts had known provenance and had been documented in the state's documentation effort, and several were lovely, small Amish quilts. Sarah tried everything she could think of—the county historical society, the state museum, the quilt museums in the region. Each organization declined her offer to take the quilts. She was about to give up until I was visiting family in the area, and she asked if I wanted them. Of course, I accepted the quilts. I have no idea what will happen to these quilts, and other antique quilts in my collection, when I am gone. The same scenario will surely play out once again.

Now, consider this scenario and apply it to old quilt tops. If the descendants don't want a finished quilt, they certainly do not want an unfinished top. Most likely, they won't know what to do with it, and the fragility of the object is problematic. It can't be used easily. In most cases, the next generation who has the job of cleaning up the closet floor will find little to no value in that old top.

I firmly believe that if an old quilt top is finished, it stands a much-greater chance of being valued in the future. If the quilt has a label and even the slightest bit of provenance, its value increases even further.

TOP LEFT: A block from a pattern known as Grandmother's Flower Garden photographed at Havenly Farm, Fulshear, Texas

TOP RIGHT: Detail image of a newly finished top, circa 1850s.

WHAT DO THE EXPERTS SAY?

DON'T RUIN IT

I recommended not finishing the quilt on *Antiques Roadshow* for two reasons. First, it was an original design, and second, when I am in a public setting giving advice, I lean conservatively. I think you have to consider several factors before you finish a quilt. Is it old and rare with so much value that you do not want to "ruin" it? Everyone has a different threshold.

—Dana Balsamo, AQS Certified Quilt Appraiser, Licensed Auctioneer, and Textile Appraiser for *Antiques Roadshow*, Season 29 and 30

GO FOR IT

Finishing is better than leaving something tucked away. Also, people are more likely to display a finished quilt because it can be put on a bed and there is a layer to fold back and look at. It becomes very usable. Lately, I've seen machine-quilting patterns that bring out so much detail and beauty to that old top, and seeing those finished quilts has given me a new perspective. I've become more open-minded.

—Antique dealer Cindy Rennels, Cindy's Antique Quilts

An exhibition of my quilts at the International Quilt Museum at the University of Nebraska, Lincoln. The quilts were on view from June through October 2025 in the museum's third-floor conference area.

When antique experts talk about the monetary value of an object, they typically do not take this very real question about the object's next life into consideration. They are looking at the object only at that moment in time. They are studying the age of the quilt top, the technical quality, and the beauty and originality and appraising it as it stands in that moment. But then what? Where does it go? What is its next life? The number of museums and historical repositories willing to take these quilt tops is extremely limited.

"Let's say you stumble upon a quilt top made by Eleanor Roosevelt. Machine-quilting a vintage or antique quilt top that is historically important would all but destroy its original inherent value," notable antique-quilt expert Julie Silber told me. "All the quilts in between? The ones that have no historical value outside of a family—to each her own."

I absolutely agree. There are certain quilt tops that have a pristine historical value that should not be altered, but these are extremely rare. Julie goes on to say, "As a dealer in vintage and antique quilts, my particular customers would, for the most part, reject an old top that has been newly machine-quilted." For an antique-quilt dealer, machine quilting an old top drastically changes the value in a negative way. The object becomes something that is not as sellable as a pure antique quilt. But most quilters are not finishing old quilts tops in order to sell them. We are making them for enjoyment.

Well-known quilt appraiser and auctioneer Dana Balsamo appeared on the beloved *Antiques Roadshow* television program. In a clip from one episode, Dana advised the owner of an unfinished antique quilt top not to finish the top, but to leave it as is. The owner happened to be a quilter, so this was an important instruction from an expert appraiser.

"I recommended not finishing the quilt on *Antiques Roadshow* for two reasons. First, it was an original design, and second, when I am in a public setting giving advice, I lean conservatively. I think you have to consider several factors before you finish a quilt. Is it old and rare with so much value that you do not want to 'ruin' it? Everyone has a different threshold. A Double Wedding Ring, a Dresden Plate, and even kit quilt tops are not rare and typically not very old. Maybe the top is valued at $100. I would be fine finishing those. But someone else might find that valuable. I would not recommend finishing a Baltimore Album quilt top, a signature or name inscribed quilt top, or other rare example," Dana Balsamo said. Dana is an AQS- Certified Quilt Appraiser, Licensed Auctioneer, and Textile Appraiser for *Antiques Roadshow*, Season 29 and 30.

Xenia Cord, of Legacy Quilts, says there are two problems with machine-quilting an old top. "The action of the machine needle may result in perforations to the fabric itself—creating a 'tear on the dotted line' effect. Second, manipulating the host fabric may inversely affect the tension to the new thread and may stress the fabric and its flexibility."

These points are fair and valid. However, in my experience of finishing dozens of old tops, I have never seen the machine needle make tears in the fabric. Today's needles are incredibly sharp and well designed. Their ability to do their job effectively is amazing, especially if you replace the needle with every project as I do. As to Xenia's second point, yes, this happens. Sometime there is stress on the seams, or along the appliqué edges, that is created as the machine stitches the layers together. I'm always mindful of this. If I observe stress on the patchwork and the underlying piecing stitches start to show, when possible, I machine-quilt over those compromised seams. In this way, I know the seams are secure forever. As I do this, I feel I am actually making the top stronger, not compromising it, because a machine-quilted top is not going to fall apart.

Cindy Rennels has been an antique dealer for decades. After operating Cindy's Antique Quilts for so long, Cindy has come full circle on her thoughts about machine quilting. "For me, this question has taken a lot of different turns and twists. I do approve of it for most part," she explained to me in an interview. "Finishing is better than leaving something tucked away. Also, people are more likely to display a finished quilt because it can be put on a bed and there is a layer to fold back and look at. It becomes very usable. Lately, I've seen machine-quilting patterns that bring out so much detail and beauty to that old top, and seeing those finished quilts has given me a new perspective. I've become more open minded."

Keeping an open mind is so important. I say bring the old tops out of the closet and off the shelves. Finish them. Enjoy them. And celebrate them while you give them new life.

HAND VERSUS MACHINE

Let's go back to that situation where the antique dealer refused to sell me a quilt top that was intended to be machine-quilted. In her mind, hand-quilting that top would be okay, but the machine was unacceptable. Because the majority of old tops are pieced by hand, many people feel that means the three layers should also be finished by hand.

Let's also remember that not all tops are hand-pieced, of course. Sewing machines were popular home appliances beginning as early as the 1850s!

I've heard from countless quilters who tell me that they have an old quilt top, but they are afraid to machine-quilt it because they feel a responsibility to finish it only with hand-stitching. If hand-quilting is a skill you have, and you have the time and motivation to do that, then hand-quilting is an excellent way to finish these tops. Hand-quilting is soft and beautiful, and the process can be very relaxing. I was a hand quilter for the first fifteen years of my quilting life.

However, in the Western world, very few of us hand-quilt anymore, and the time it takes is daunting. So in reality, we never get started on these old tops. Instead, they sit unfinished waiting for that special day in the future when you are going to start hand-quilting this top. In the future, we always think we will make time for things like this, but mostly the future will be just as busy as today. In my view, finished by machine is better than sitting on the floor of the closet unfinished.

I think the thing that holds us back the most is fear, myself included. Many quilters worry they will make mistakes and thus harm the value of an old top. They worry that their machine-quilting skills are not up to the task. I am often reminded of a quote by Sheryl Sandberg: "What would you do if you weren't afraid?" My advice is to keep moving forward. Set those fears aside. If you approach finishing your quilt top with love and enjoyment, everything will be fine.

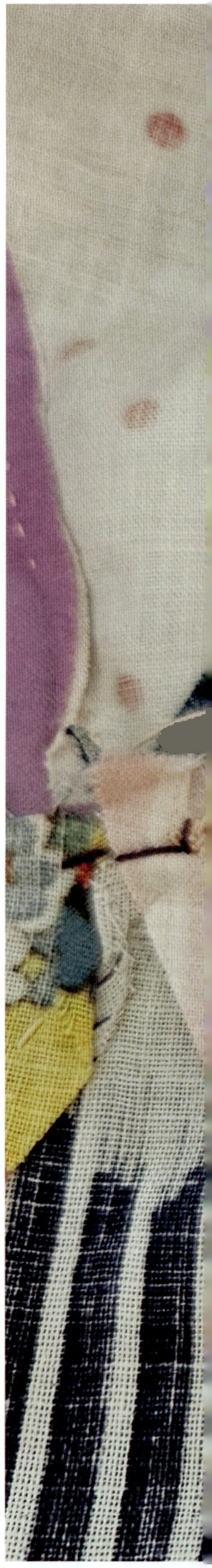

Most antique quilt tops are hand-pieced, as opposed to today, when handwork in the Western world is not popular.

EDUCATION: LABEL THAT QUILT!

Reprinted with permission from the Quilt Alliance.

LABELING IDEAS FOR QUILTS YOU MAKE

The sky's the limit when you're labeling your latest quilt. Remember, not every label has to have every item below—but when it comes to labeling quilts, more is more!

INFORMATION ABOUT YOU:

- **Your name:** Include as much of your name as you'd like, including family names or any nick-names you go by.
- **Other makers' names or recipients' names:** Who else helped make this quilt? Did you use a longarm service? Was the quilt made as a gift for someone?
- **Location:** Where the quilt was finished, started, or worked on, or where you live.

I treat the labeling process as a secondary creative outlet.

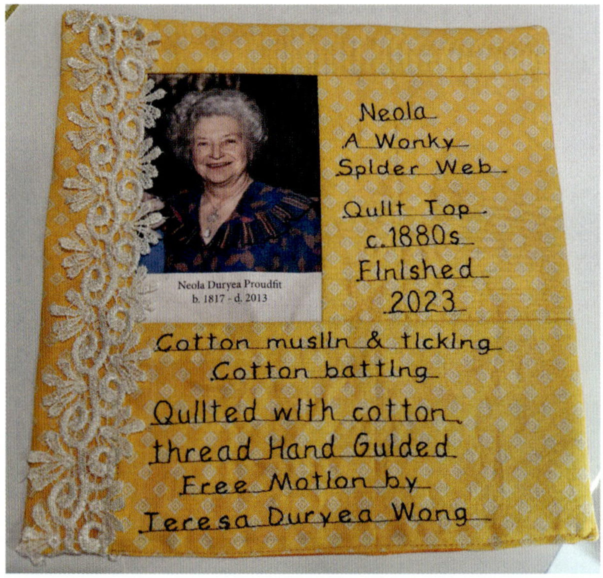

- **Why you made this quilt:** Was it for a quilt show? A gift? To use up a certain fabric? To practice a technique after taking a class? To experiment? What inspired you?
- **What else is happening in the world or in your world:** For example, "made during the COVID-19 pandemic" or "made as healing quilt after Steve's illness."

I treat the labeling process as a secondary creative outlet. Ribbons and fun fabrics can make your labels more interesting. I also often include photos printed on cotton on my home printer. The lettering is created using the alphabet setting on my domestic sewing machine, but you can also handwrite the information, or even hand-embroider it.

Labeling your quilt is an important way to keep its history from fading away.

INFORMATION ABOUT THE QUILT:

- **Date:** Typically, the finish date, but you can also include the date you started—sometimes they're decades apart.
- **Title of the quilt or quilt pattern:** Whether it's a published pattern or your own creation.
- **Materials and technique:** This might include type of fabric/fiber, fabric designers or collection names, thread and betting details, cost of fabric (quilts are historical documents!), number of stitches, hours spent on the quilt, etc.
- **Photos:** Of you, of the recipient, of the quilt's inspiration, or anything else.
- And more: Care and washing instructions, thank-you notes, exhibition information, whether the quilt is part of a series . . . and anything else you might want to include.

LABELING IDEAS FOR QUILTS MADE BY SOMEONE ELSE

Do you have a family quilt, a quilt you purchased, or a gifted quilt without a label? Add a label to it today! This can feel difficult if you don't have a lot of information. Write down everything you think you know, and indicate if it's something you're sure about or just an educated guess.

- **Date:** When you received or purchased the quilt or when you think it might have been made (on the basis of family history, information from the seller, or your own research).
- **Location:** If you know (or suspect) the location where it was made, include it. Also include the location where you acquired the quilt.
- **Who made the quilt:** If it's a guess, that's okay! For example, you can say "said by my family to be made by my great-grandmother Effie Barnes. She lived from 1901 to 1971. She changed her last name from 'Parker' in 1932, so it was made sometime after that year."
- **Any other information about the quilt that you received or know about:** Include it! Even if it's a guess or something you're not sure about, write that down; it's okay to say "maybe" or "probably."

PRO TIPS:
TO WASH OR NOT TO WASH

Let's start with antique or vintage quilt tops. For me, the answer is that I never wash them. I feel they are too delicate, and washing could put stress on the seams or appliqué. Instead, when I'm shopping in person, I look for quilts that are clean and do not smell. When shopping online, I have to trust the seller's description that the quilt top does not smell and is not heavily stained.

Others are willing to take this risk and wash old quilt tops. One of the tops that was gifted to me had been washed in a washing machine, and it survived, but there was a ton of thread on the back where the seams had unraveled. It took a couple of hours to neatly cut it all off.

As for small spots, stains, or discoloration, I am willing to accept these are part of the charm of these old quilts. I am often reminded of a beautiful quote from one of Japan's renowned quilters, and a woman I was fortunate to spend a bit of time with over the years, Shizuko Kuroha. In her forty-plus years of quilt making, Shizuko used only old, antique fabrics for her quilt tops. She passed away in 2024 but loved bringing these old textiles to life, and she was brilliant at it. When I once asked her about stains or discoloring, she said, "Well, those spots are just another color." Her wisdom makes me smile.

When it comes to washing a finished antique quilt, I am open to the idea. But it is not something I can recommend, because there are too many variables that can change the outcome.

This is the question I am asked most often. The answer is complicated and depends on how much risk you are willing to accept.

I have scoured the internet and kept a tally of recommendations and tips from antique-quilt dealers, influencers, bloggers, and those on other sites.

I found a couple of sites that treat washing like any other project, and they describe the skill level as intermediate. I thought this was hilarious. Washing is not for the faint of heart. However, if I were to assign a skill level to washing, I would say that expert skill is needed.

HERE IS THE INTERNET'S CONSENSUS:

- **Before you jump in, try vacuuming the quilt first. To do this safely, lay a fine screen over the quilt. Tape the edges to avoid any snags. Vacuum over the screen. This protects the fibers in the quilt. You can also hang the quilt outside for some fresh air. Either of these tips might allow you to avoid washing.**
- **Handwashing is preferred. However, some experts say that the machine on a delicate cycle, or rinse only, will work just fine. If handwashing, there are some excellent tips that suggest first**

lining your bathtub or sink with a plastic tarp to protect it from any bleed in the colors. Lay a sheet under the quilt before you handwash it so you can lift the wet quilt out with the sheet and thus avoid putting stress on the quilt.

- There is a wide discrepancy in what kind of detergents to use. I found several recommendations for OxiClean, Soak, or Orvas. Woolite is often discouraged. Adding a small amount of distilled white vinegar to the water is also often recommended.
- When handwashing, do not wring or agitate the quilt. Rather, pat it gently to ensure it is fully soaked. Some experts say a ten-minute handwash is fine; others say two hours. Rinse completely.
- Most experts recommend laying the quilt flat to dry. Never hang it to dry, since this will put too much stress on it.

> *Consider those old spots as just another color.*
>
> *—Beloved Japanese quilter Shizuko Kuroha*

ABOVE: I washed this antique quilt in the machine on delicate cycle, with cold water. I also placed it in the dryer but removed it while it was still slightly damp and laid it flat. This process was risky. The colors could have faded or bled, and the seams could have been compromised. But I wanted to use this quilt on the couch. Ordinary quilts like this one are meant to be used, after all. So, I was willing to accept the risks. If it was ruined, then so be it. Fortunately, it survived just fine and smells lovely, and it's now soft and cuddly.

FREE MOTION TIPS FOR FINISHING OLD TOPS

HOW TO BUILD CONFIDENCE WITH FREE MOTION

I was never good at drawing. If you ask me to draw a person or an animal on a piece of paper, it will look ridiculous. But I can make a series of doodles on paper. And I can create patterns and shapes with continuous lines and curlicue motifs.

Interestingly, continuous lines and curlicue motifs are the skills used most often in free-motion quilting. Creating them with a sewing machine is not all that different from drawing on paper. With practice and patience, you too can create your own hand-guided, free-motion quilting motifs, without the use of a computer.

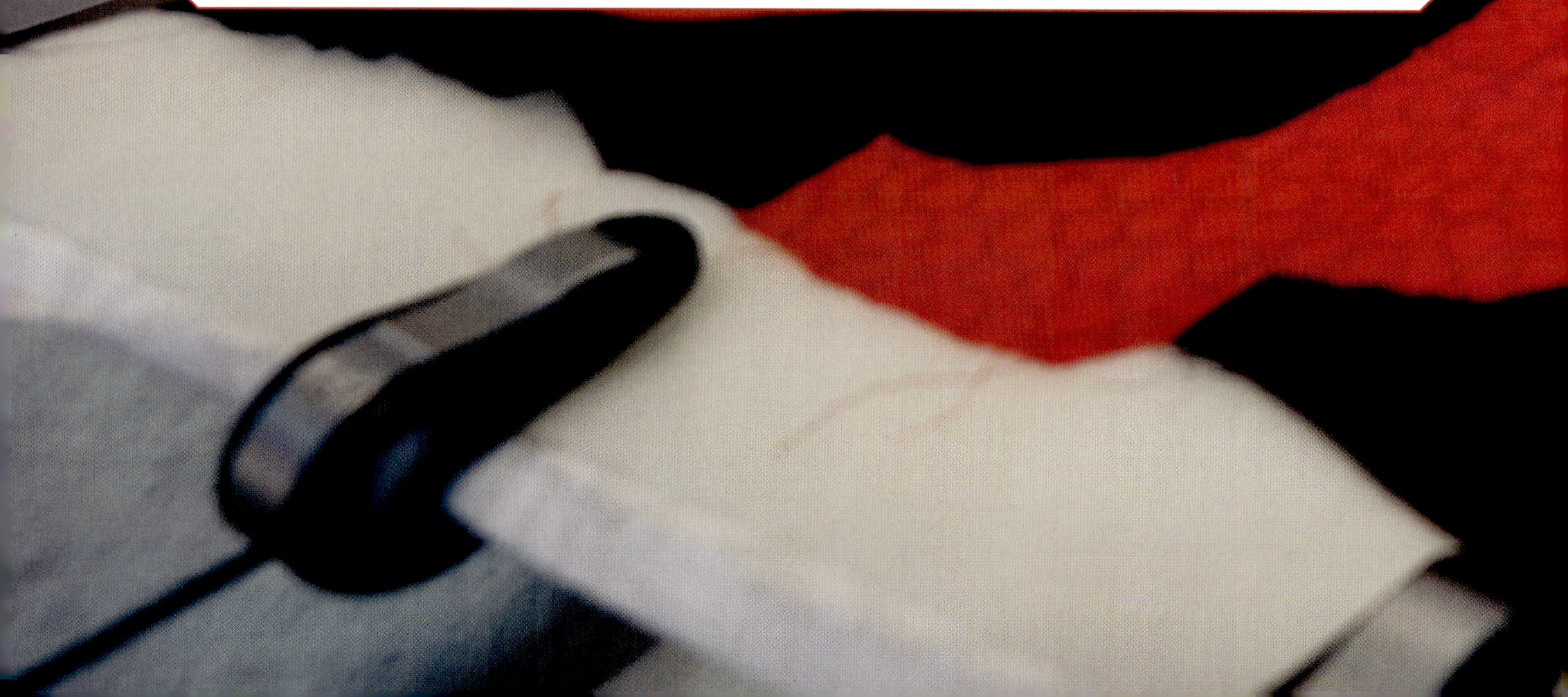

The author in her studio with an antique quilt top loaded on the frame with a Bernina Q24 longarm quilting machine. Photo by Jimmy Wong.

ABOVE AND OPPOSITE: Debbie Schulze is a professional longarmer based in Taos, New Mexico. This is one of the many preprinted panels she has finished that show off her artistry. The title is *Blazing Glory*. Debbie is an also an accomplished quilt maker, but in between quilt making, she occasionally turns to these colorful panels as an outlet to express her creativity.

A FEW TIPS TO GET STARTED

- One of the most important tips I can offer is to let go of the idea of perfection. From my perspective, quilting is not about being perfect. Rather, it is an art form to be enjoyed and so therefore the process should also be free of judgment and be enjoyable. In my stitches, you will not find perfection. But you will find a lot of love.
- Start small. Make a simple patchwork quilt and practice quilting it with free motion. You can always give the quilt away or use it as a dog or cat bed.
- Quilting on preprinted panels is an excellent way to practice free motion. You can add a border to these panels and practice your quilting, and then it makes a nice gift to give away.
- Honor the patchwork. Stitch one motif in each piece of patchwork and vary the motif in each patch. In other words, do not quilt an overall (or edge to edge) design. Practicing in one small patch, or block, can help build skills while simultaneously creating a gorgeous quilt.
- Embrace the seam ripper. No other art form has such an incredible tool where we can just erase our mistakes and go on. I've spent hours ripping free-motion stitches. And that's okay. I learned what not to do, and then I can start over with a clean slate.

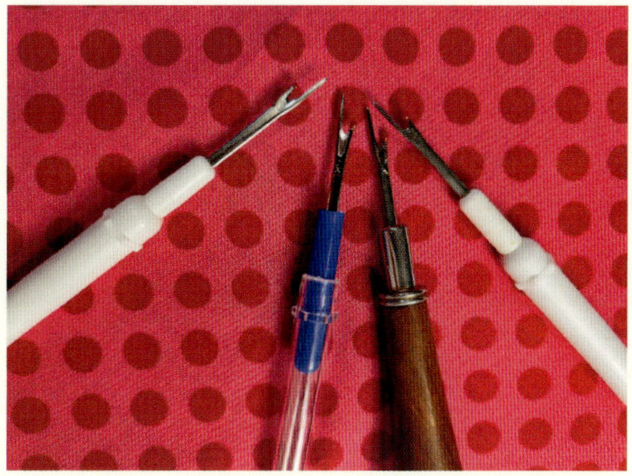

- Keep breathing! It's easy to get nervous and focus all of your attention on the outcome. Try not to think too far ahead, and just enjoy the rhythm of the machine and the amazing stitches being created right in front of you.

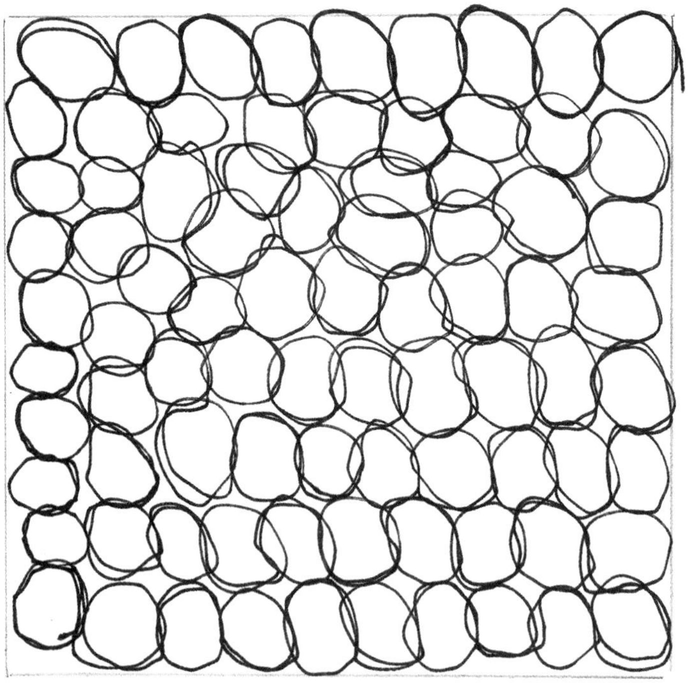

BUBBLES

FLAME

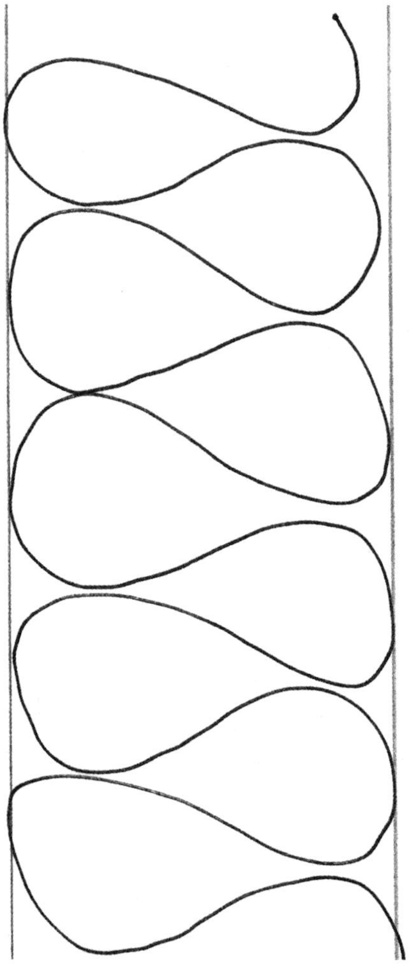

RIBBON

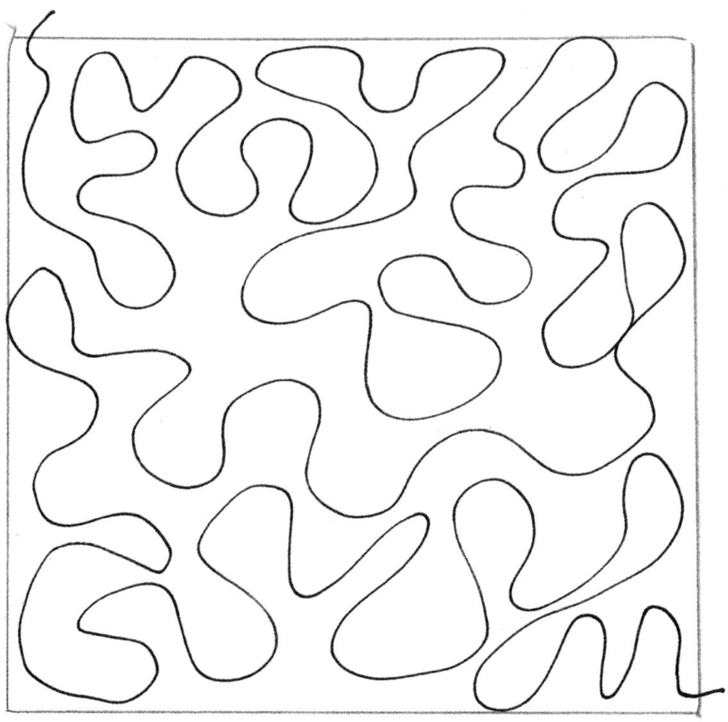

STIPPLING

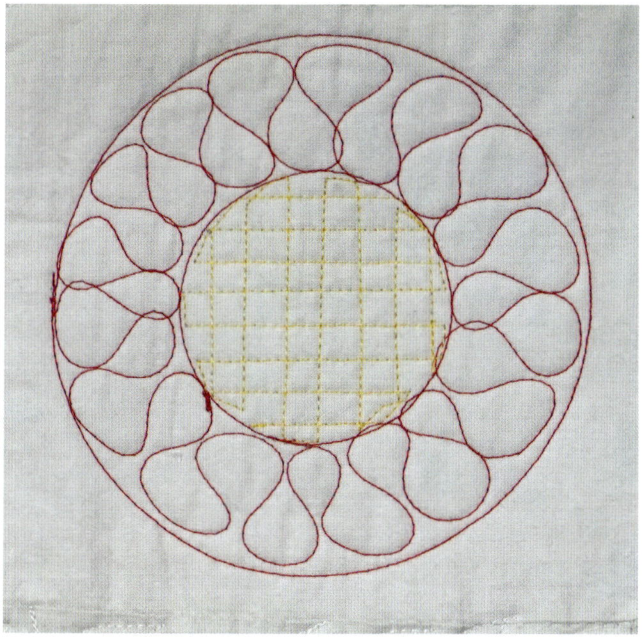

Example of the ribbon motif surrounding a circle with a ¼-inch grid.

FOUR MOTIFS TO LAST A LIFETIME

My favorite motifs are the ribbon, flame, bubbles, and stippling. I find stitching these four motifs to be relaxing and fun.

On the ribbon and flame stitches, the stitch is achieved by guiding the machine with a gentle back-and-forth motion, almost like sitting in a rocking chair. It is a great filler for borders or sashing. It is also easy to master and looks great on a quilt.

The key to the gently swaying lines in the flame motif is to make a sharp point at the tip.

Smooth swirls over and over are used to make the ribbon stitch. You can vary the look by touching the sides or even overlapping the swirls.

Example of the flame stitch.

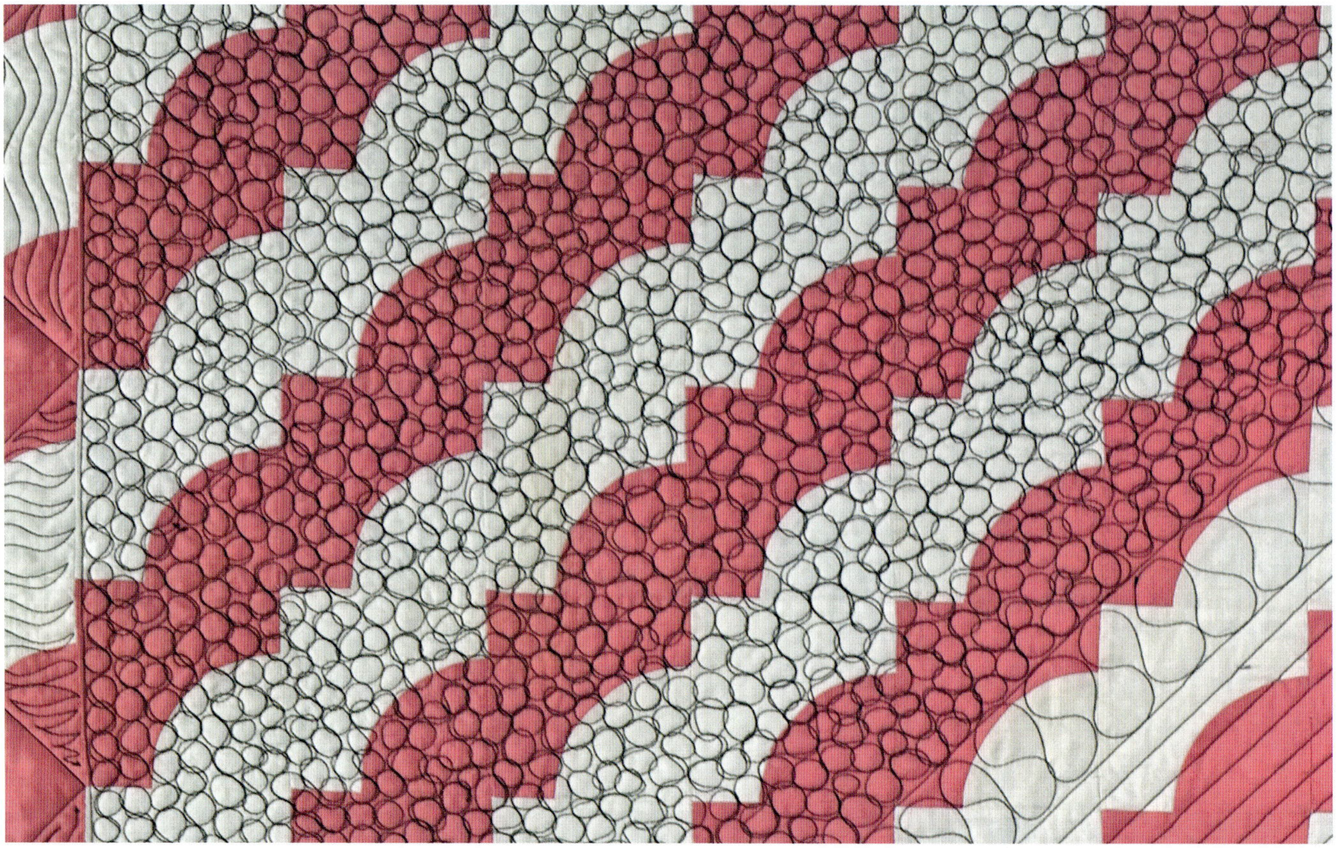

The bubble motif can work just about anywhere. Go slow to create smooth circles, but again, do not try for perfect circles. Imperfections in this motif just add to the artsy effect. If you get stuck in a corner area, you do not have to stop stitching. Instead, just travel back around the edges of the same circles to get the machine positioned in the next area where you want to stitch.

You can keep all the bubble sizes the same for uniformity, or you can vary the sizes to create a different pattern.

The motif known as stippling is a classic. Keep the lines gently swerving. Do not make abrupt moves or sharp angles. In addition, it looks better if the lines never cross.

RULERS RULE

If you have a longarm machine, try using commercial quilting rulers. These are shapes made from a ¼-inch-thick acrylic. You will need a free-motion foot on your machine that has a thick base that is appropriate for using rulers. Also, invest in a table attachment for the machine that fits snugly around the needle compartment. This attachment will allow you to hold the rulers steady while stitching.

There are a plethora of great ruler shapes on the market, and I have a drawer full of them. Rulers are a fun way to create designs and patterns that you might not otherwise think of. For example, you can use a ruler to create a perfectly shaped circle or oval, then you can fill it in with your own hand-guided motifs. It is the best of both worlds. Many of the rulers can be applied in a multitude of ways that create professional patterns and designs.

OPPOSITE, TOP: This example shows a combination of motifs in each patch. The light-green flower print is stitched with a basic stippling. The purple patch next to it shows stippling, with the addition of small loops. Bubbles fill the red patch, and ribbon stitches were created to fit the triangle shape in black/white-stripe print.

OPPOSITE, BOTTOM: Endless bubbles are fun to stitch and look great.

RIGHT: Commercial quilting rulers were used to create perfectly shaped half circles in this inner border. Next, I filled in the half circles with a free-motion ribbon motif.

LEFT: This example shows matchstick quilting with tight spacing, as well as a separate section where the lines are spaced slightly farther apart. Varying the width of the lines can create distinct patterns. In addition, the bubble and ribbon motifs were also used here.

HOW TO START AND STOP—OR SHOULD YOU REALLY BURY THOSE THREADS?

The most professional method of dealing with the threads at the start and stop of every movement is to bury the ends of the threads at the beginning and the end of every line (or section) of stitches. If you are creating quilts that will be judged in a competition, this is the recommended technique. Burying the threads creates a beginning and ending stitch that is clean and nearly undetectable. The end result of these clean stitched lines can be stunning.

However, I rarely do this. I choose not to spend hours burying loose threads in my quilt. I understand that doing so makes a beautiful start and stop, and I admire those quilters who take this step. My preference is to begin each stitch with a tiny backstitch and to end with a tiny backstitch. Then I pull up the bobbin thread to the top and cut the loose threads. Yes, the backstitches are visible if you are examining the stitching. For me, making a backstitch is quicker and allows me greater enjoyment over the process. Having a backstitch visible is perfectly fine with me. You should try both methods and decide what works best for you.

ANYONE GOTTA MATCH(STICK)?

Matchstick quilting is quilting in straight lines that are stitched very close together. Typically, the lines are a ¼ inch apart, or they can be even closer. Matchstick quilting can travel over appliqué or pieced sections, or these can be used in the negative spaces.

If the quilt is an improv style with irregular seams, I will create matchstick quilting organically with no ruler. In this case, the slight imperfections in my stitched lines pair well with the improv piecing. If the quilt is more traditional or features precise seams, straight lines created with a ruler can be effective fillers. My go-to ruler for matchstick quilting is a 10-inch straight ruler. There are much-longer rulers available, but I find them difficult to hold steady. The 10-inch ruler seems to fit my outstretched hand better and is easy to hold steady. For matchstick lines that are longer than 10 inches, I stop and move the ruler. There is a risk that the line might not be perfectly straight, because when you move the ruler it might create a jagged stitch within the line. This is a choice I make because the smaller ruler is easier to hold, and therefore more enjoyable. For me, a long acrylic ruler is stressful, and I prefer the more enjoyable path over the path of perfection. You can practice with different rulers and find your own way.

Another excellent technique for creating perfectly straight lines on a longarm is to use the locks, or controls, on the machine that enable you to move the machine in one straight line across the quilt top. I use this function often if I am creating horizontal matchstick lines, or a grid, over the entire quilt. To create matchstick lines that travel across the entire quilt, always travel in the same direction for each line—either left to right, or vice versa. I do not recommend traveling back and forth with long straight lines, because it can create puckers in the quilt top.

For long matchstick lines that cross over the entire quilt top, begin stitching off to the side (in the extra batting) before you reach the quilt top. Travel across in one continuous line. Stop on the other side off the quilt top and end the stitch in the extra batting. By starting and stopping off the quilt top, you avoid the need to bury threads or make a backstitch.

To create a grid on a longarm, stitch the entire quilt in one direction, take it off the frame and turn the quilt 90 degrees, reload it, and stitch the remaining lines.

With matchstick quilting, the question of whether you should bury the threads becomes more problematic, especially if you are stitching short, close lines in a small section. In the most-exquisite, award-winning quilts, the quilter will stitch only one row at a time—even if that line is very short—and the threads are buried for each short line. However, for my own quilt making, to create matchstick lines in small areas I stitch in one direction until I get to the end of the row, then I simply move the machine over to the next row while still stitching and keep stitching in the opposite direction. This leaves a tiny connecting line in alternating rows.

You can experiment with various ways to create matchstick quilting and decide which technique works best for you.

Circa 1920s, Amish quilt top known as Joseph's Coat or Bars.

WORKING WITH OLD QUILTS

One of the most challenging aspects of finishing old quilt tops is the fact that many of them do not lie flat. The fabrics used to make these old tops have changed over time. Many of them have stretched. Another factor is that many old quilts were created using a lot of muslin. When muslin is stitched to cotton and then left to sit for seventy-five years, it usually creates havoc.

If you are using a longarm or a domestic machine, do not make the mistake of thinking you can flatten it as you go. This rarely works.

Ironing and steaming the quilt top can help it lie flat. But sometimes, you might have to do some repairs. Occasionally, patches can be easily removed, especially muslin, and then reassembled in order to make the top lie flat. But this can also open a can of worms—meaning that if you fix one block, then every other block might need to be fixed as well. To be honest, the degree to which I am willing to do repair is limited, because I'd rather invest my time quilting, not repairing. Instead, I look for quilt tops that lie flat, or ones that need just a bit of tweaking. I do not want to spend several days fixing an old top. But everyone is different, and if you have the patience to do that, it can be very rewarding, especially if the quilt was made by someone in your family and you can save it!

As I pointed out in the description of *Marie's World*, I had an ongoing fight with that quilt top for weeks and weeks. It was very wavy, and all the methods I employed to fix it did not work. In the end, I made a couple of small tucks in the quilt top while it was on the longarm frame and just quilted right over them. As a professional, this is not something I should recommend. However, in real life, you do what you need to do. For me, that finished quilt is one of my favorites. I love how I stitched it, and I am very proud of the fact that this old top that was just sitting around—and now, tucks and all—it is gorgeous and finished.

A PATCHWORK CONVERSATION

Throughout this manuscript, I have written over and over that my approach to quilting old tops is to honor the patchwork. What I mean by that is that I prefer to study the block and pattern design, and then I typically choose to stitch inside one small patch at a time. I feel that doing so brings each patch to life. I do not want to ignore the patchwork pattern by quilting an edge-to-edge curlicue motif that has nothing to do with the design, pattern, or color of the underlying top. This is just my personal preference.

A PLUG FOR NATURAL FIBERS

Here's my plug for natural fibers. The vast majority of old quilt tops are cotton. Of course, there are tops made with polyester and other synthetics, velvets, linen, etc. But if a quilt top is made with cotton, I am not about to finish it with polyester thread or synthetic batting. This is an extremely personal choice. Synthetics have a place in the world. Most clothing is made from synthetics, and these can be very comfortable and wrinkle-free and are adaptable to a lot of sports and activities. But as a quilt maker, I just have this strong personal preference to keep my quilt natural.

There are many beautiful synthetic threads out there; I just choose not to use them. In fact, this is a personal choice that applies to all of my quilt making, not just antique tops. The threads I use the most are 100% cotton—either 50 wt. or 40 wt.—and 100% silk.

While silk thread might be an unusual choice, it is a brilliant thread for finishing old quilts. It glides smoothly and is gentle. In addition, the quilting stitches are more subdued than thicker threads, so the overall effect adds texture without overpowering the design. Silk thread is also competitive costwise with many popular synthetic threads.

For batting, I take the same approach. I use only 100% cotton batting or 100% wool batting. I have also experimented with bamboo batting and even thin silk batting from Japan. However, my go-to batting is mostly cotton and occasionally wool. For me, these natural fibers are an important part of honoring the patchwork by adding only natural fibers.

And here is an interesting sidenote about cotton batting. Two very popular batting companies, Hobbs and the Warm Company, both purchase their raw cotton from American farmers, and their cotton batting is manufactured in America. These hardworking American farmers are growing the highest-quality cotton in the world, and that is what I choose to put inside my quilts.

Cotton harvesting in the Texas Panhandle. Photo by Teresa Duryea Wong.

WHAT'S ON THE BACK?

FIVE FAVORITE BACKINGS FOR THE BACK OF THIS BOOK

My best friend, and the woman who taught me how to quilt, Amy Gurghigian, purchased this uncut rice sacking at a garage sale, and she gifted it to me sometime around 2010. This unusual material sat in my stash for years until I found the perfect project. I used it for the backing for this Ocean Waves quilt. The sacking fabric is for the Notan rice brand, and the colors and imagery are charming.

A solid backing can be the perfect canvas to show off your machine-quilting capabilities. By using many different colors of thread and changing the bobbin to match with each thread change, the back of *Marie's World* is as beautiful as the front.

Extra-wide quilt backing is an incredible invention. There is something very satisfying about taking one large piece of cloth and loading it onto a longarm frame. When I find a great, professionally printed backing, I buy it and add it to my stash. Eventually the perfect project emerges. This backing, with these large vintage vases and the warm palette, fits well with the Thousand Pyramid quilt top. The design is by Kaffe Fassett, Free Spirit.

Old tablecloths and other vintage linens can also make great backings. This one is a vintage tablecloth I found at an antique fair. It wasn't quite wide enough, so I added solid borders on either side. The sailboat blocks in this quilt top are stitched using an extremely dense technique known as thread painting. Those layers and layers of red thread created a unique design and texture on the back.

Here's another really great extra-wide backing. It is a reproduction of William Morris by Free Spirit. This classic design and these warm cream and red colors are perfect. I could look at this backing all day.

FINALLY

And finally, here's my favorite quilt quote:

"Quilts look better when you have a lot of them."

—Famed quilt collector Joanna Rose

212

Teresa Duryea Wong is an author, lecturer, and quilt historian. A member of the International Quilt Museum advisory board, Teresa is an accomplished quiltmaker and her quilts have been exhibited in museums and quilt competitions. She has presented hundreds of presentations throughout the US and around the world, including regularly at the annual Quiltcon. She has appeared on numerous quilting programs and podcasts, including *The Quilt Show with Alex Anderson & Ricky Tims*, *Quilting Arts TV*, and *The Craft Industry Alliance Podcast*.

A contributing writer for *Quiltfolk* and other magazines, Teresa is also the author of *Sewing & Survival: Native American Quilts from 1880–2022* and books about Japanese and American quilts and textiles, and is the coauthor of *Kawaii Appliqué Quilts from Japan*. She lives in Houston, Texas.

@third_floor_quilts ▪ teresaduryeawong.com